THIS ACTIVITY BOOK BELONGS TO

....

....

All Right Reserved
Copyright© 2021 By : Art ouz

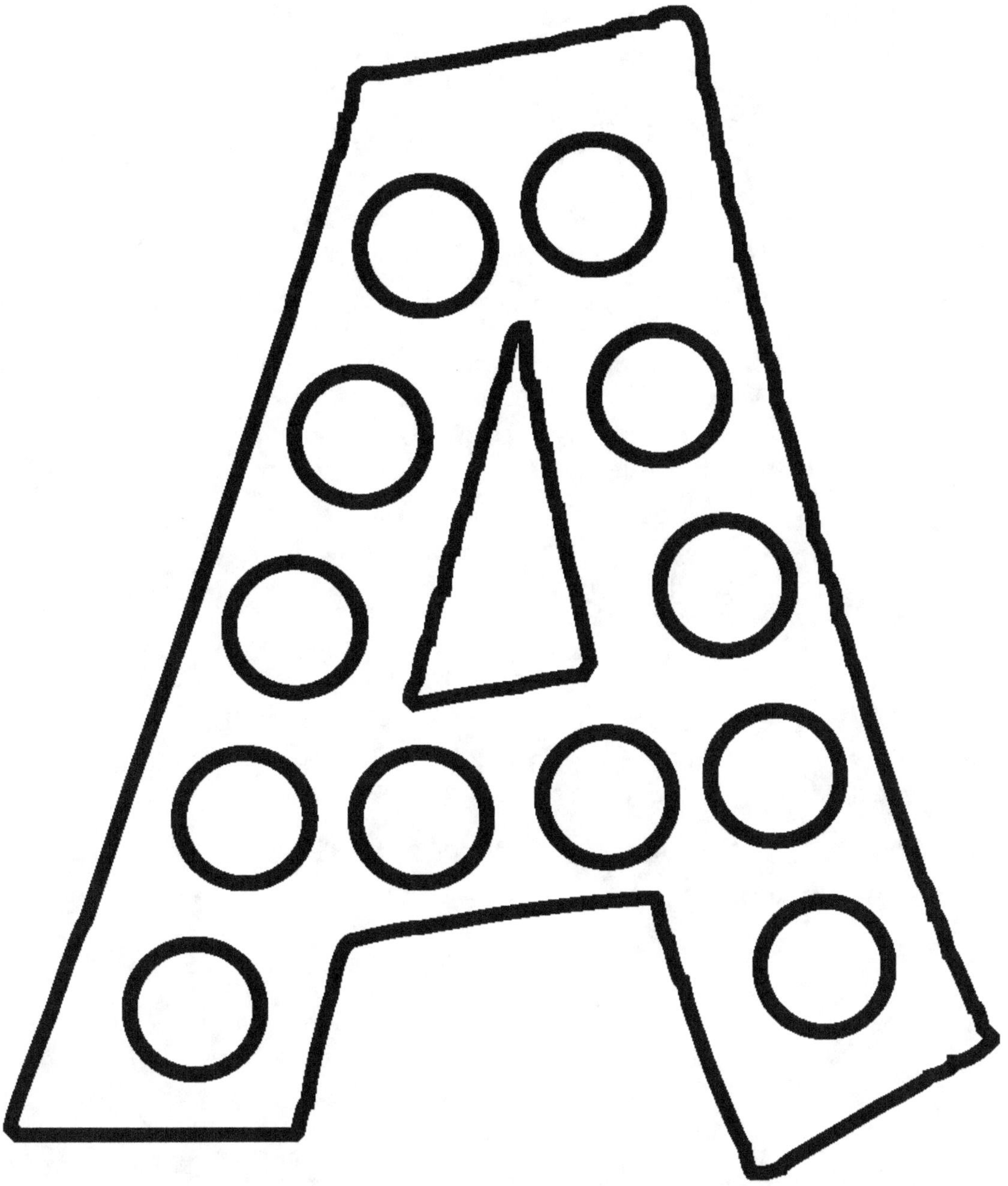

A

ALLIGATOR

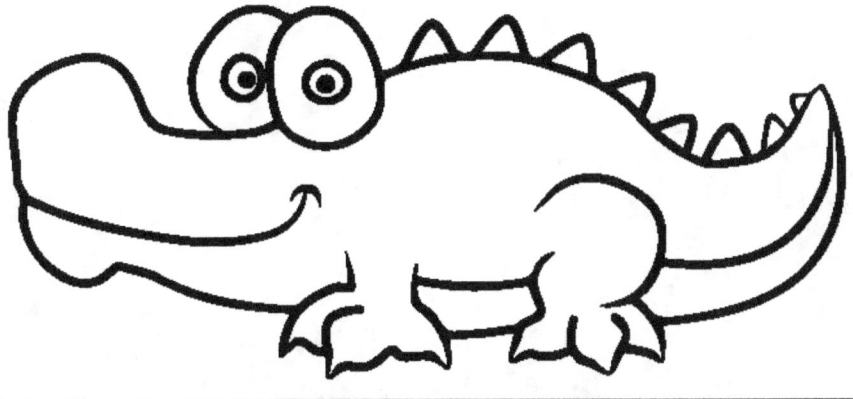

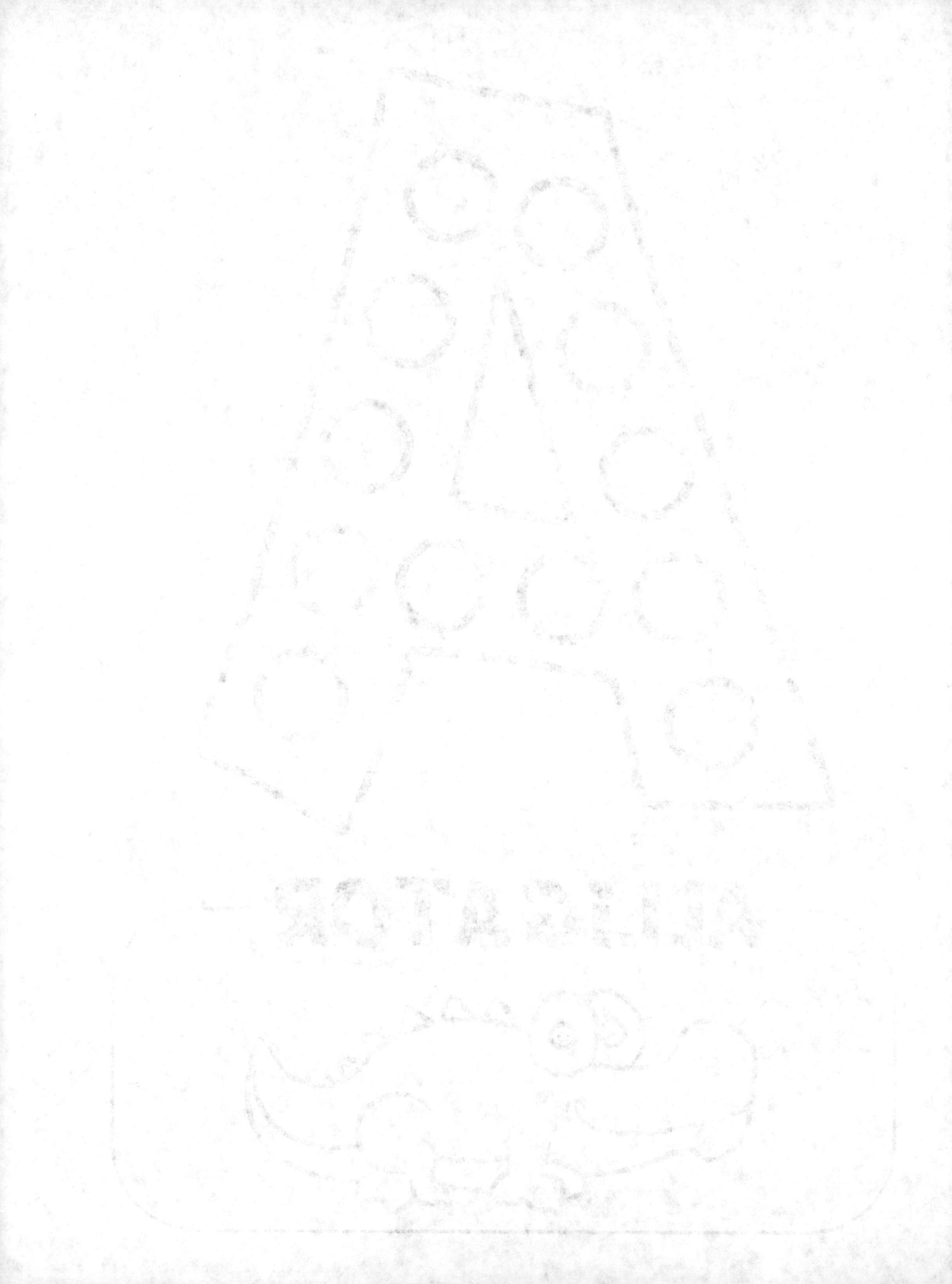

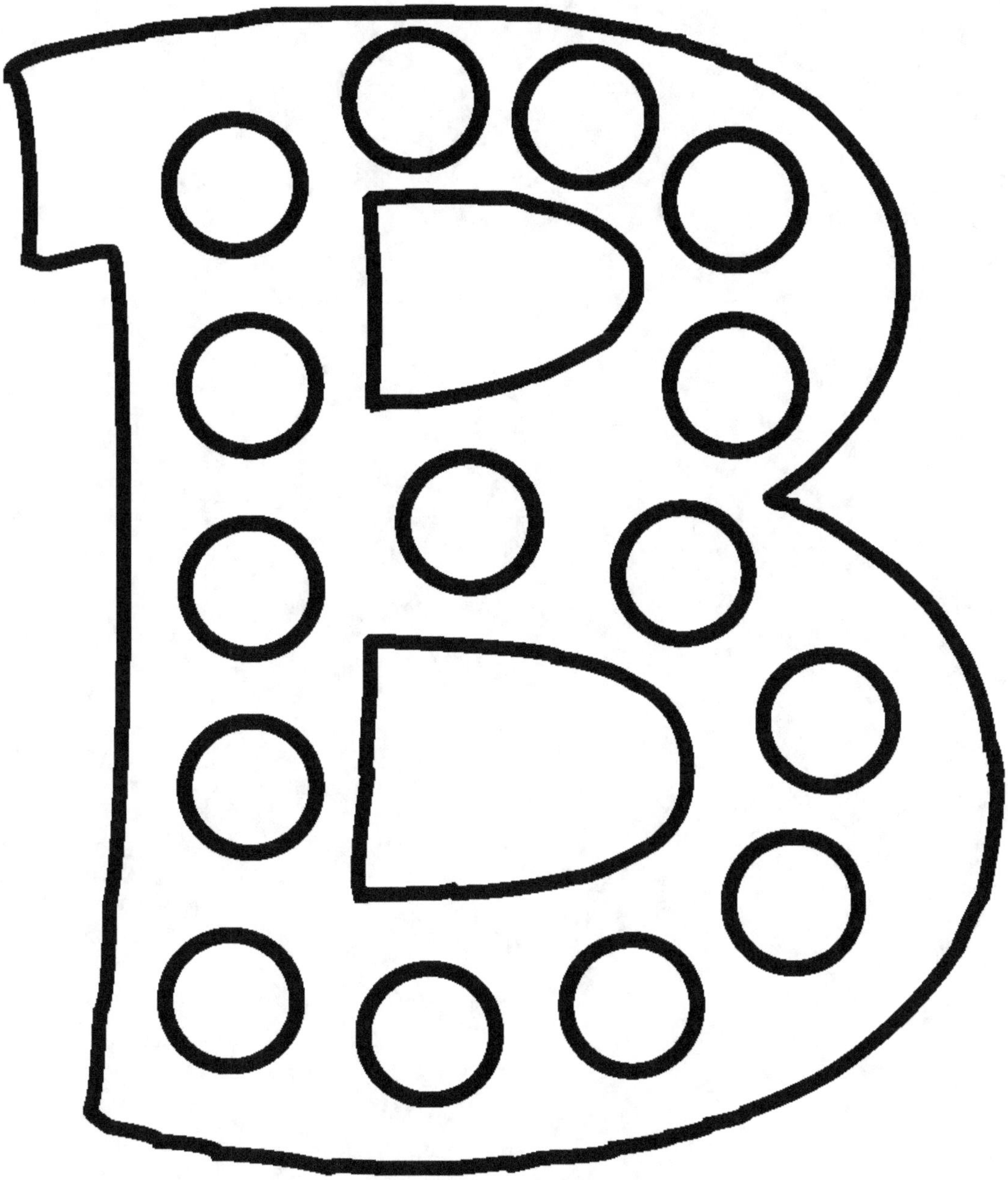

B

BiRD

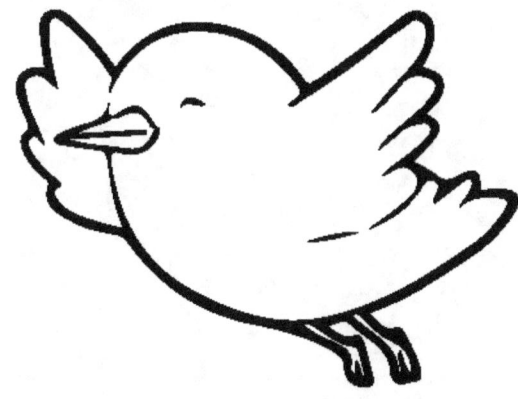

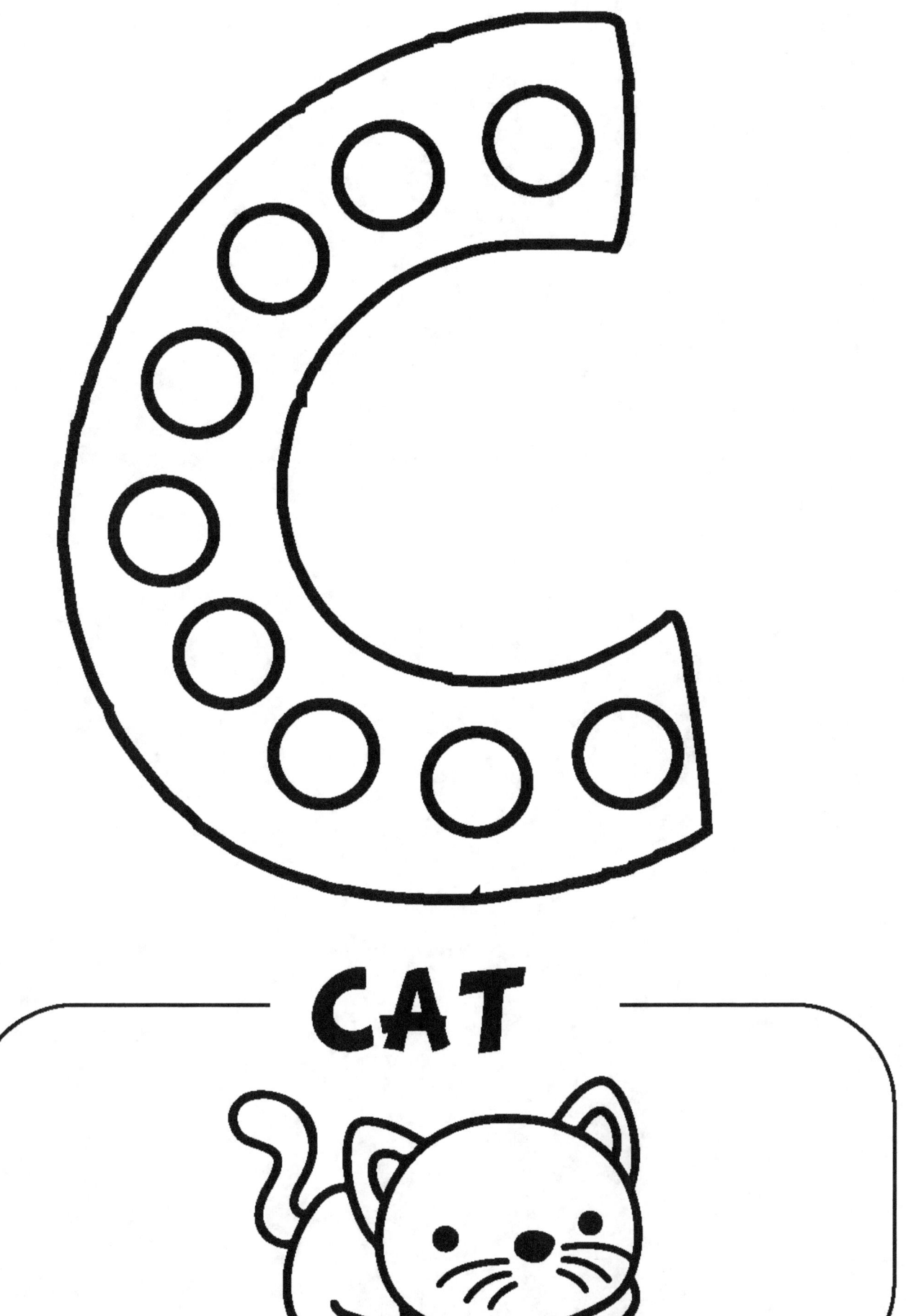

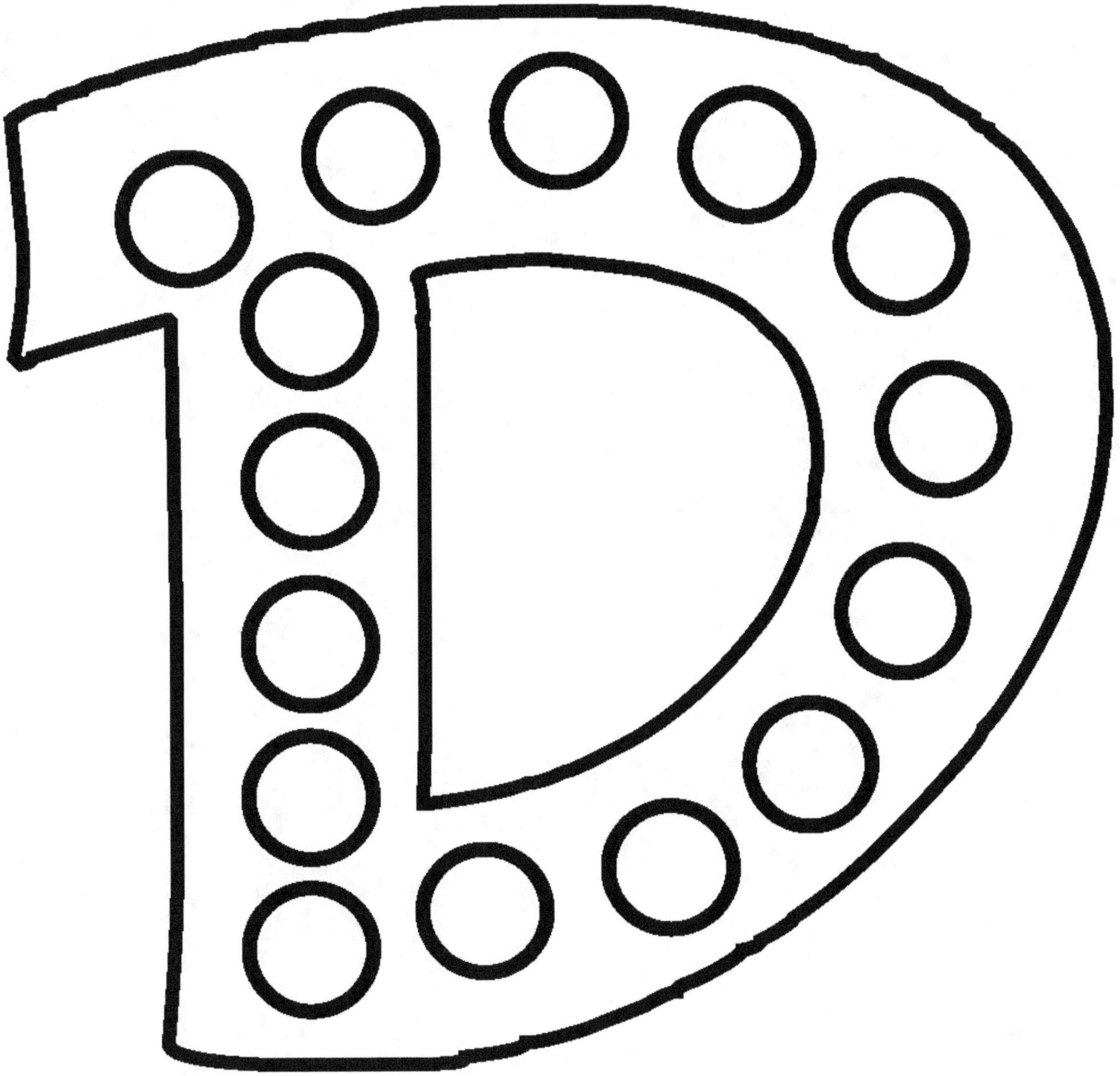

D

DOG

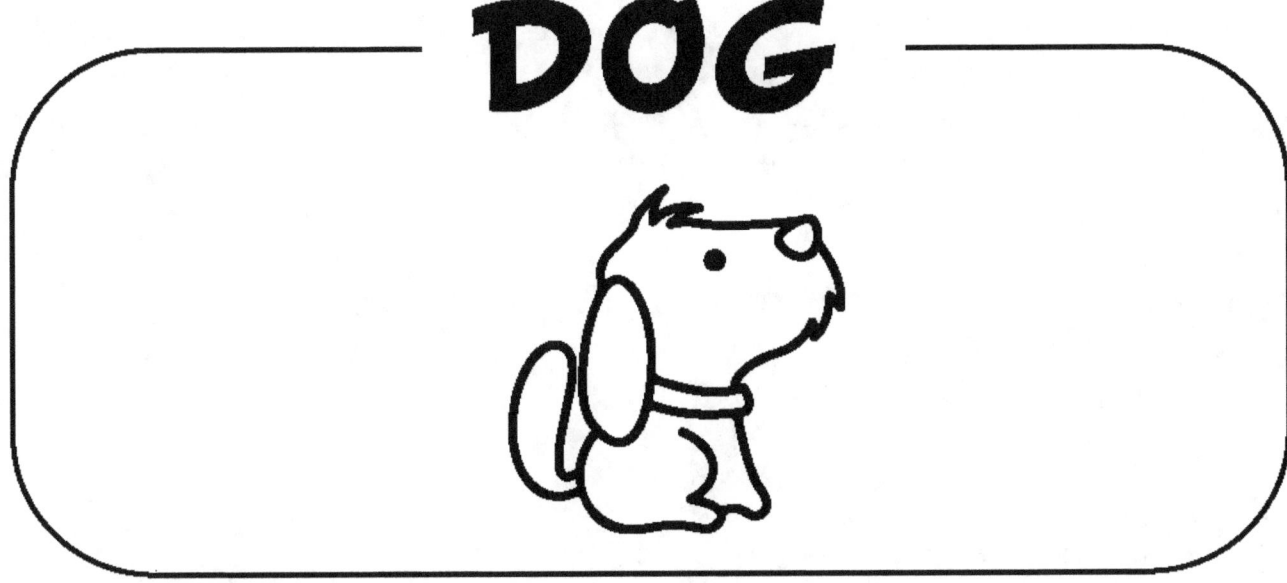

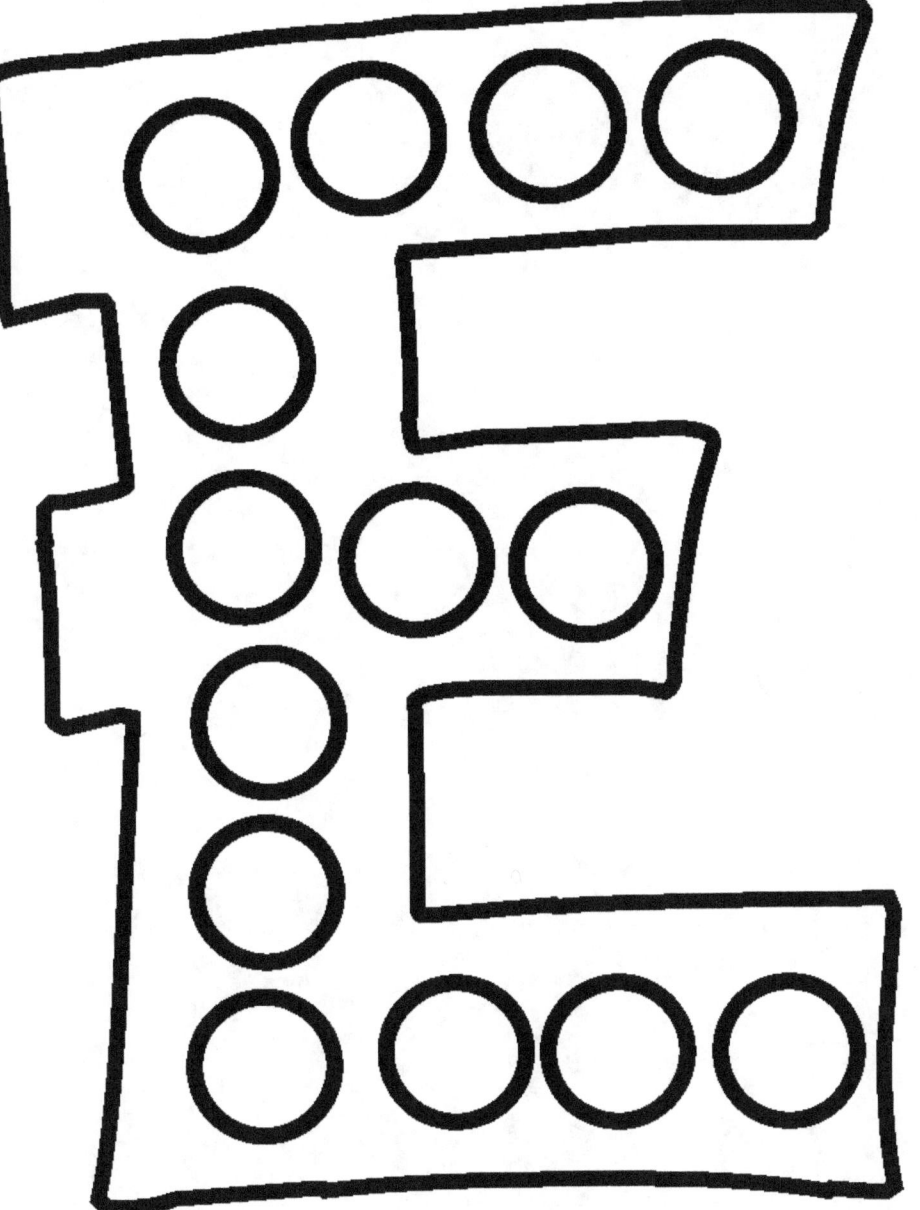

ELEPHANT

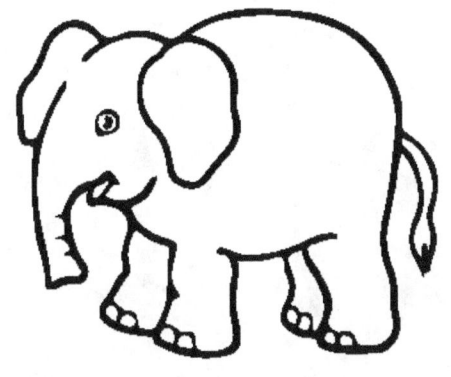

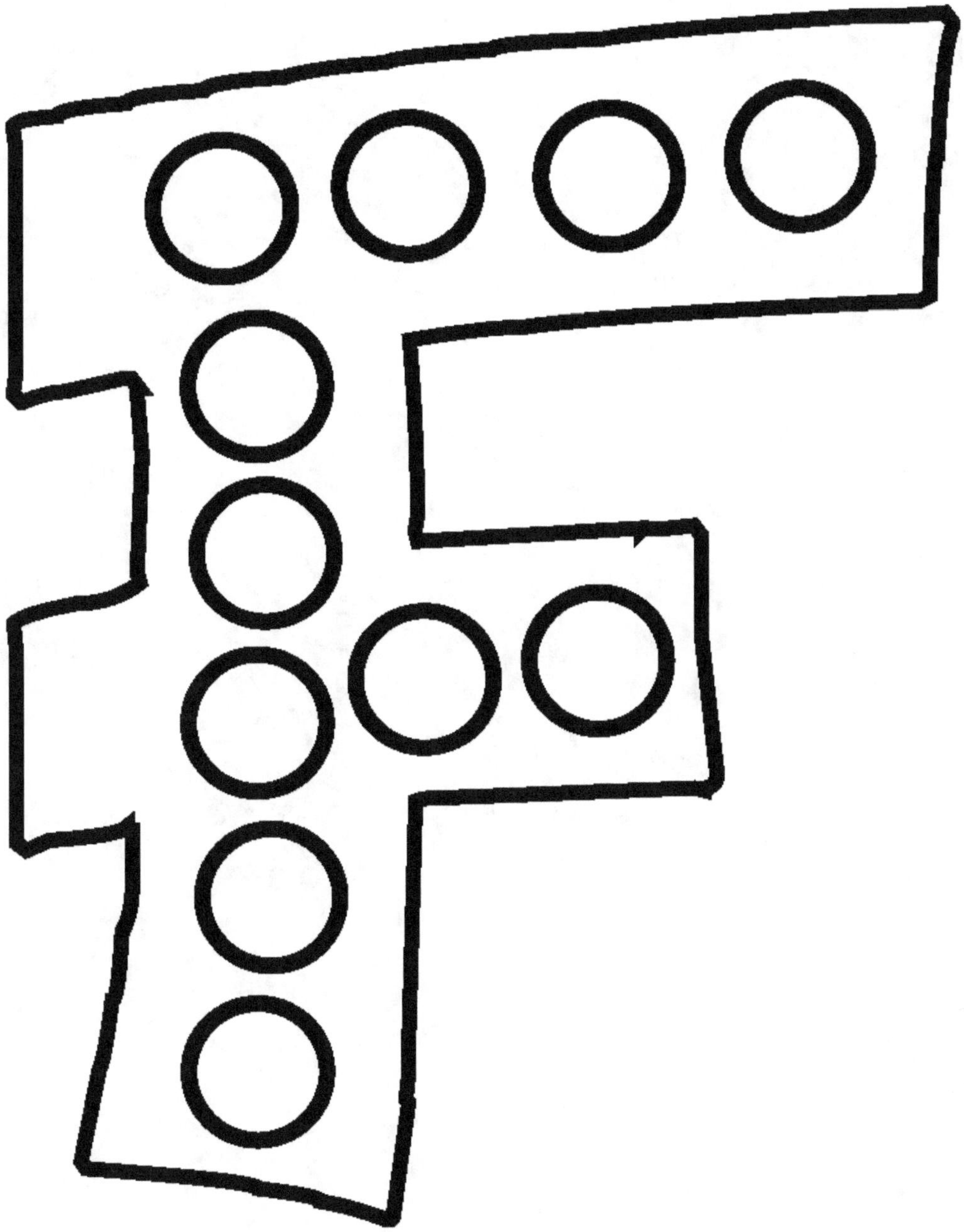

FROG

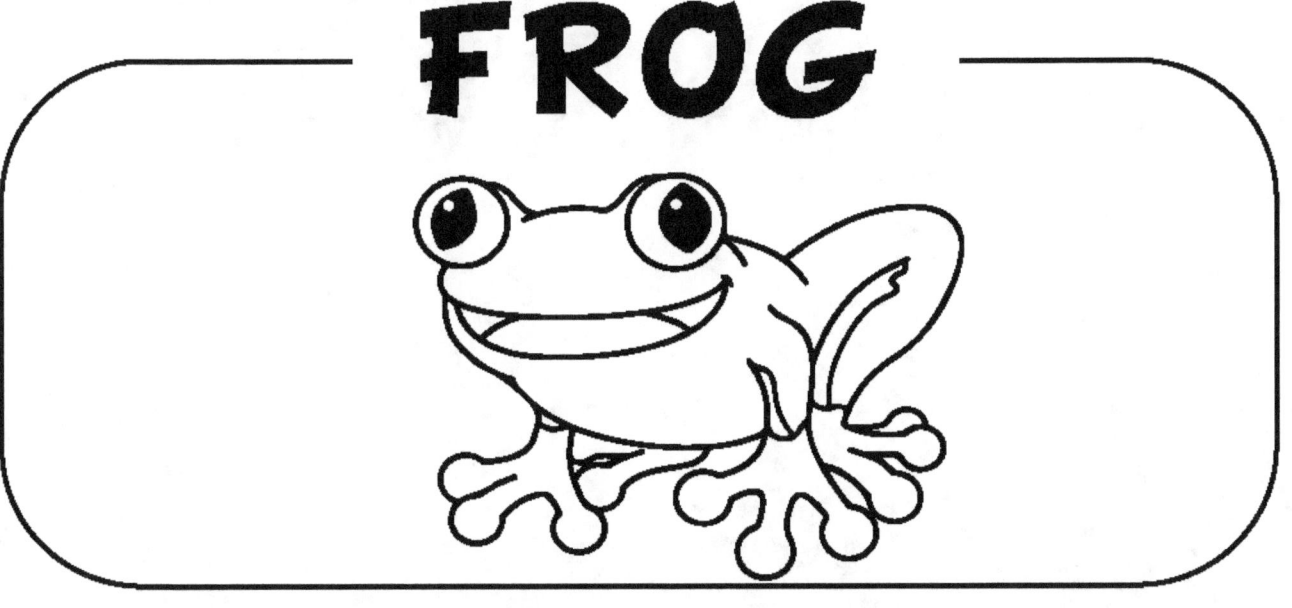

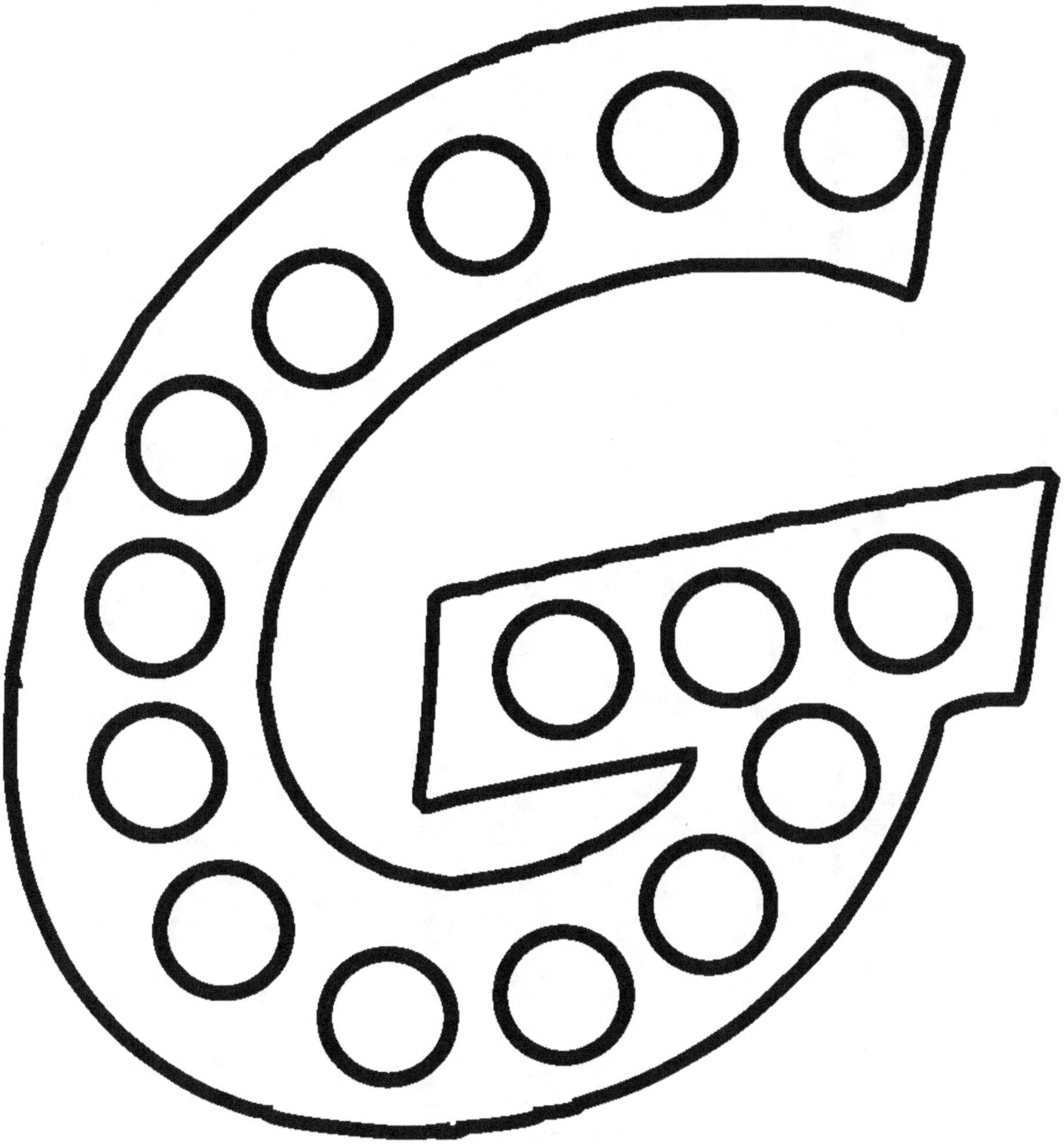

GIRAFFE

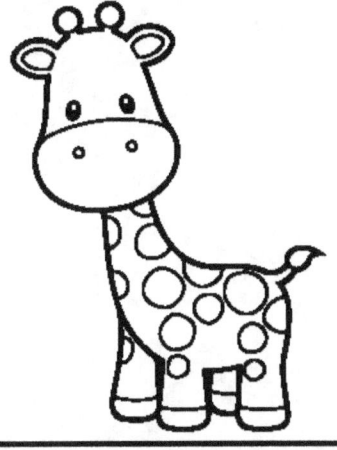

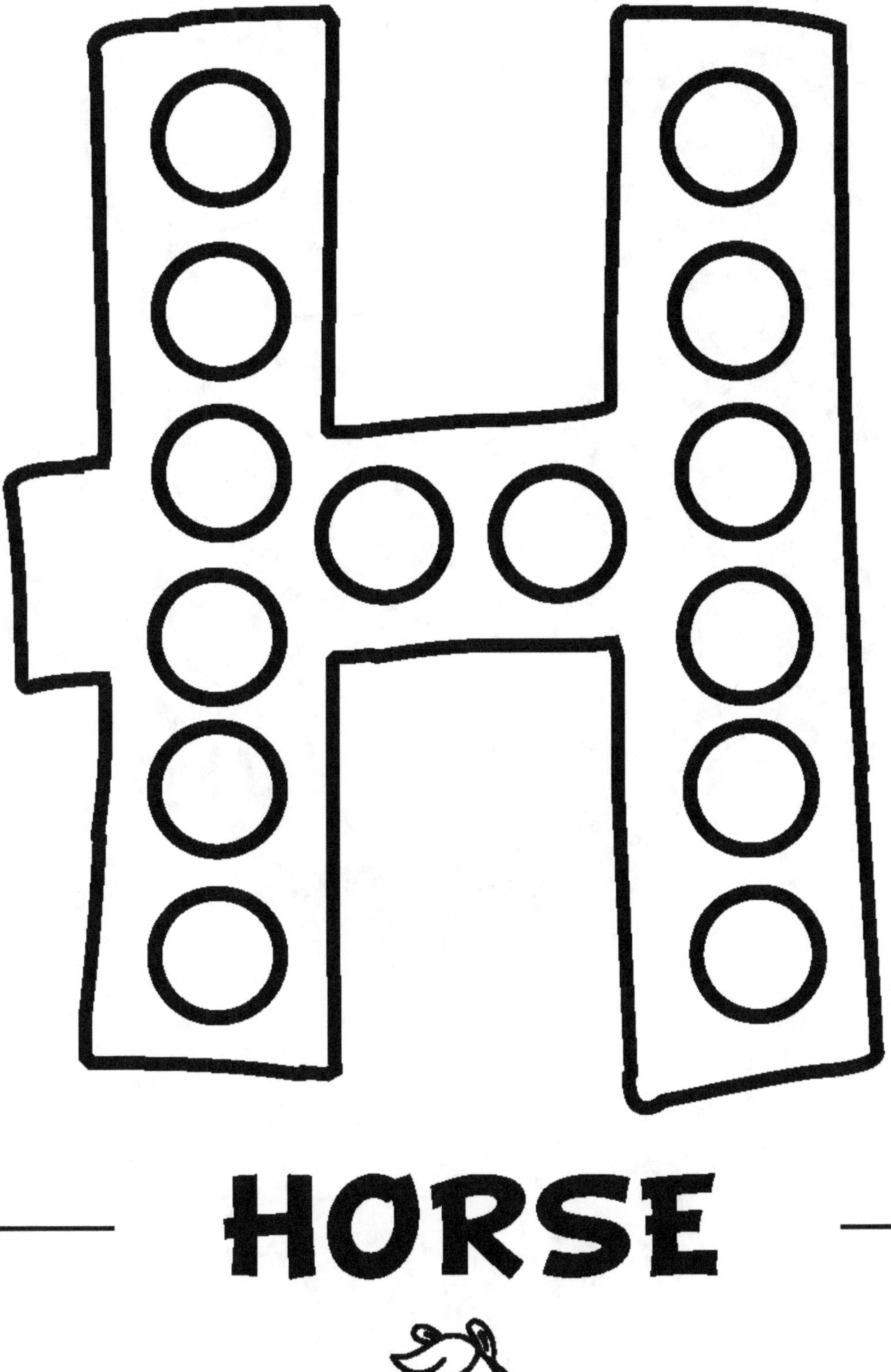

H

HORSE

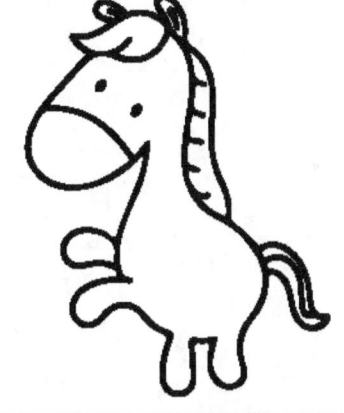

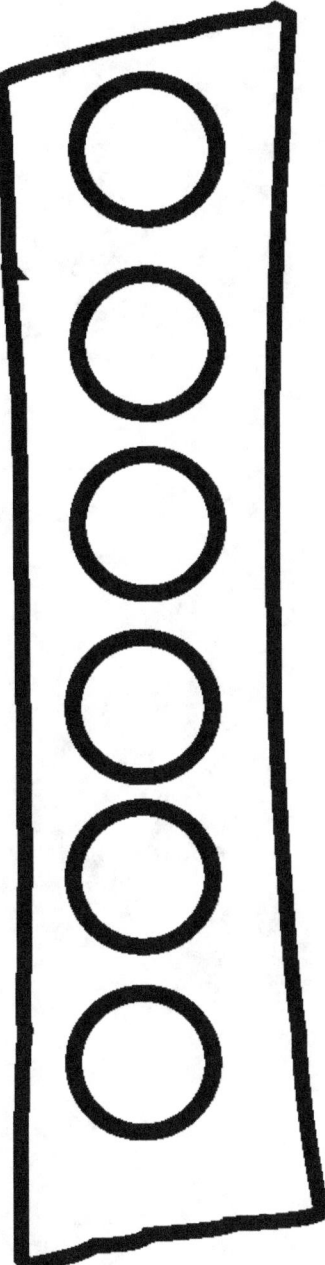

IGUANA

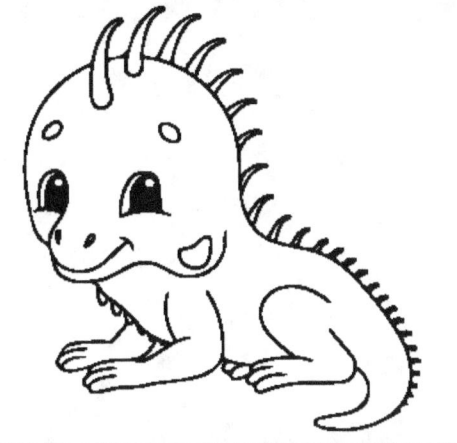

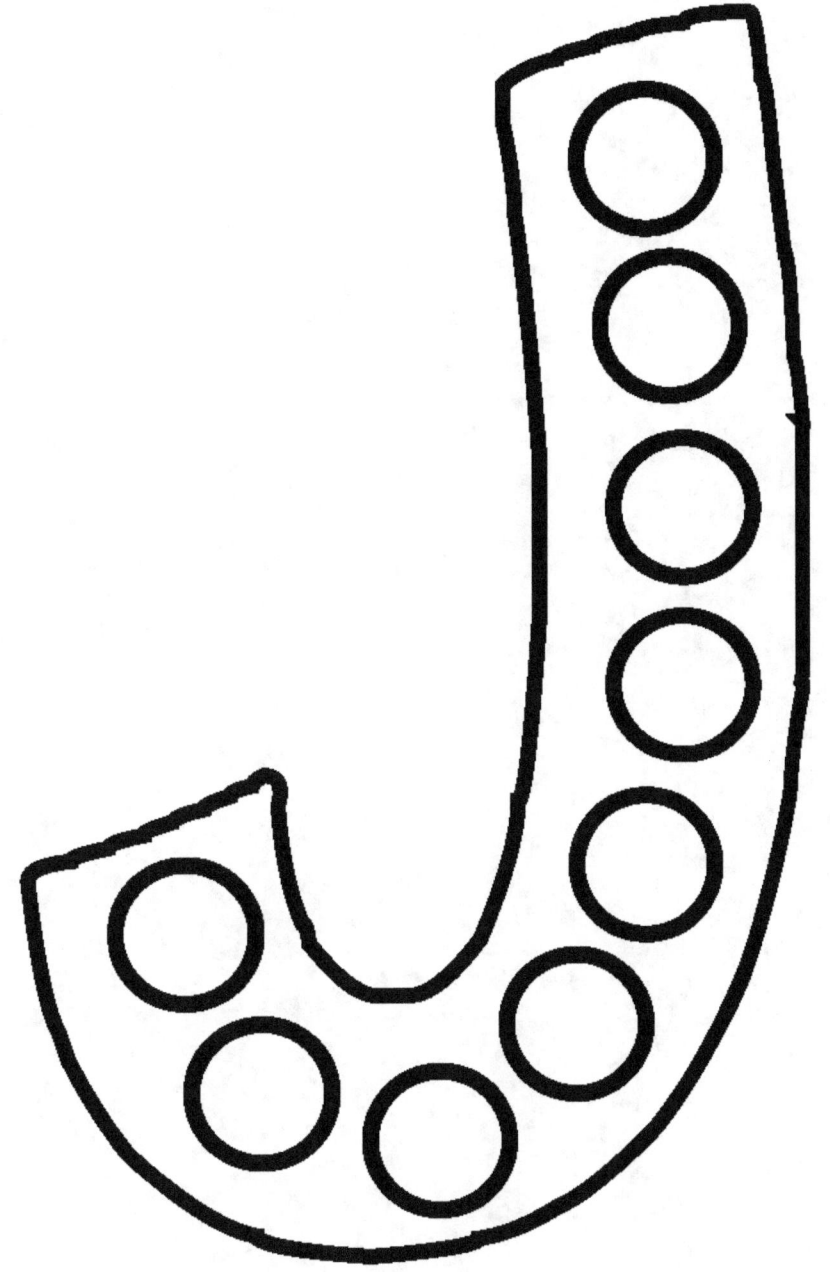

JELLYFISH

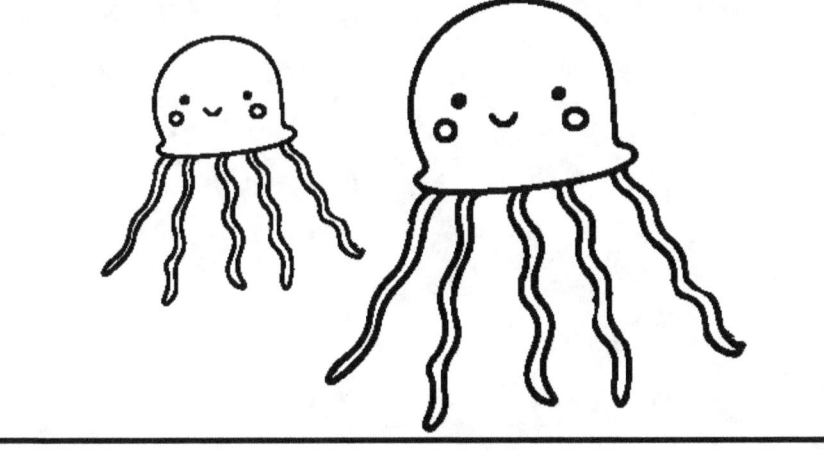

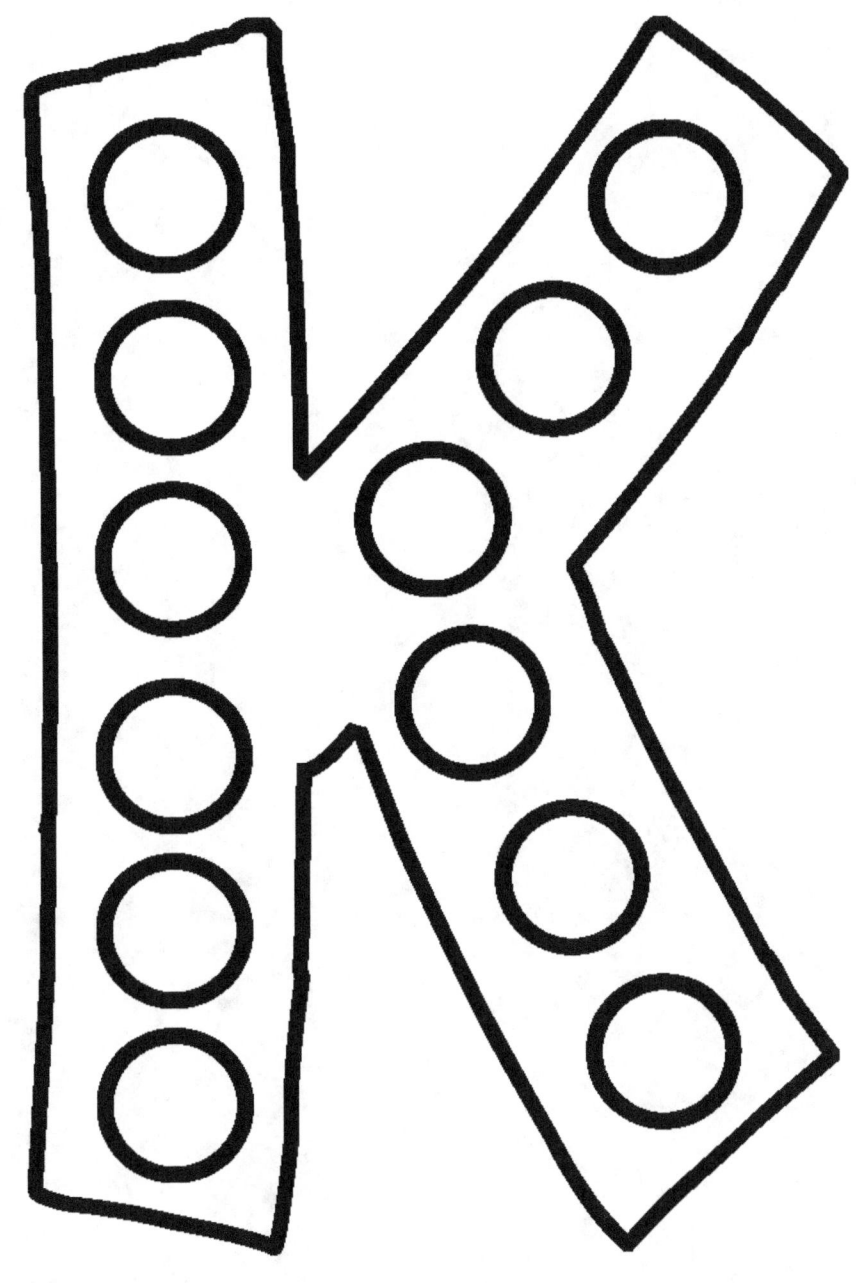

KOALA

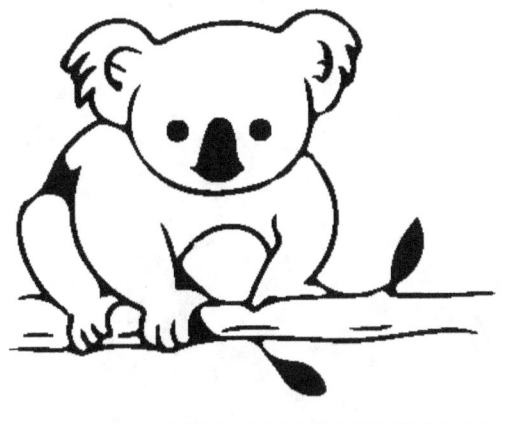

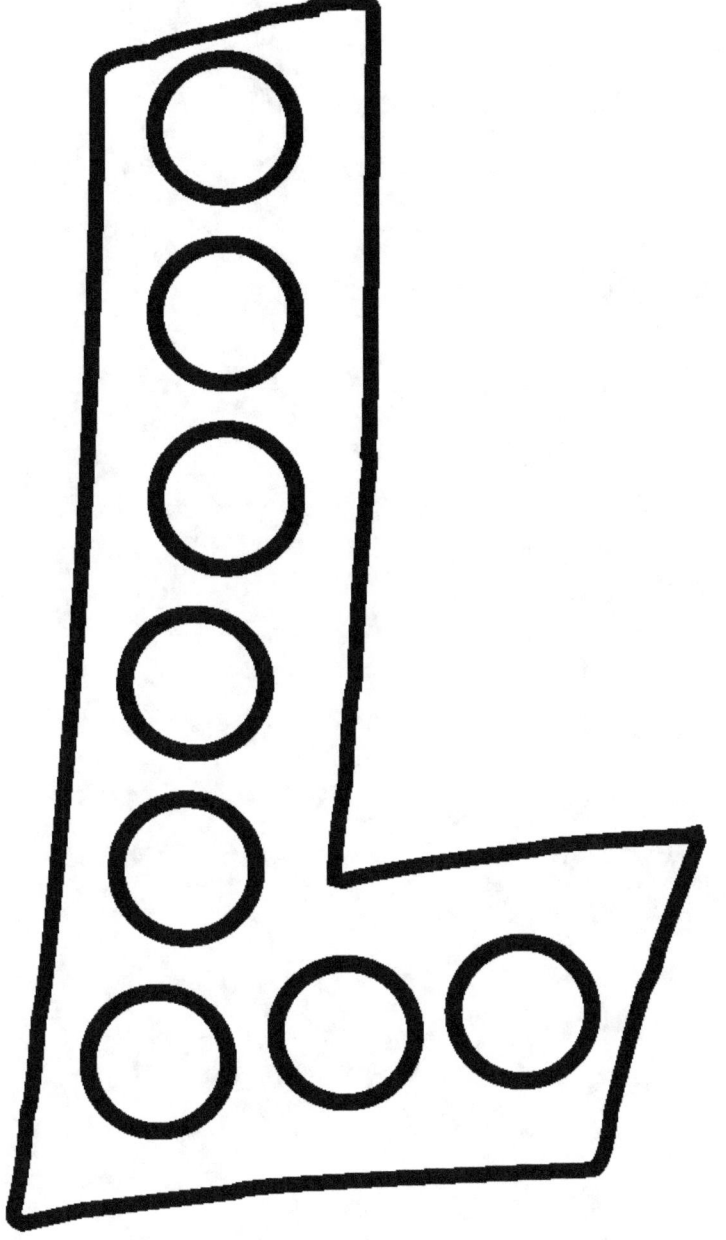

LION

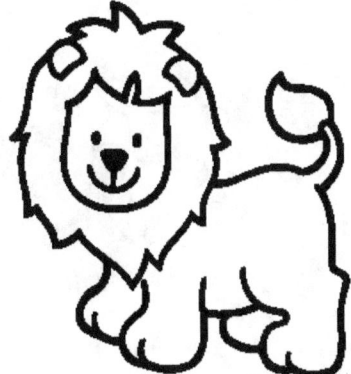

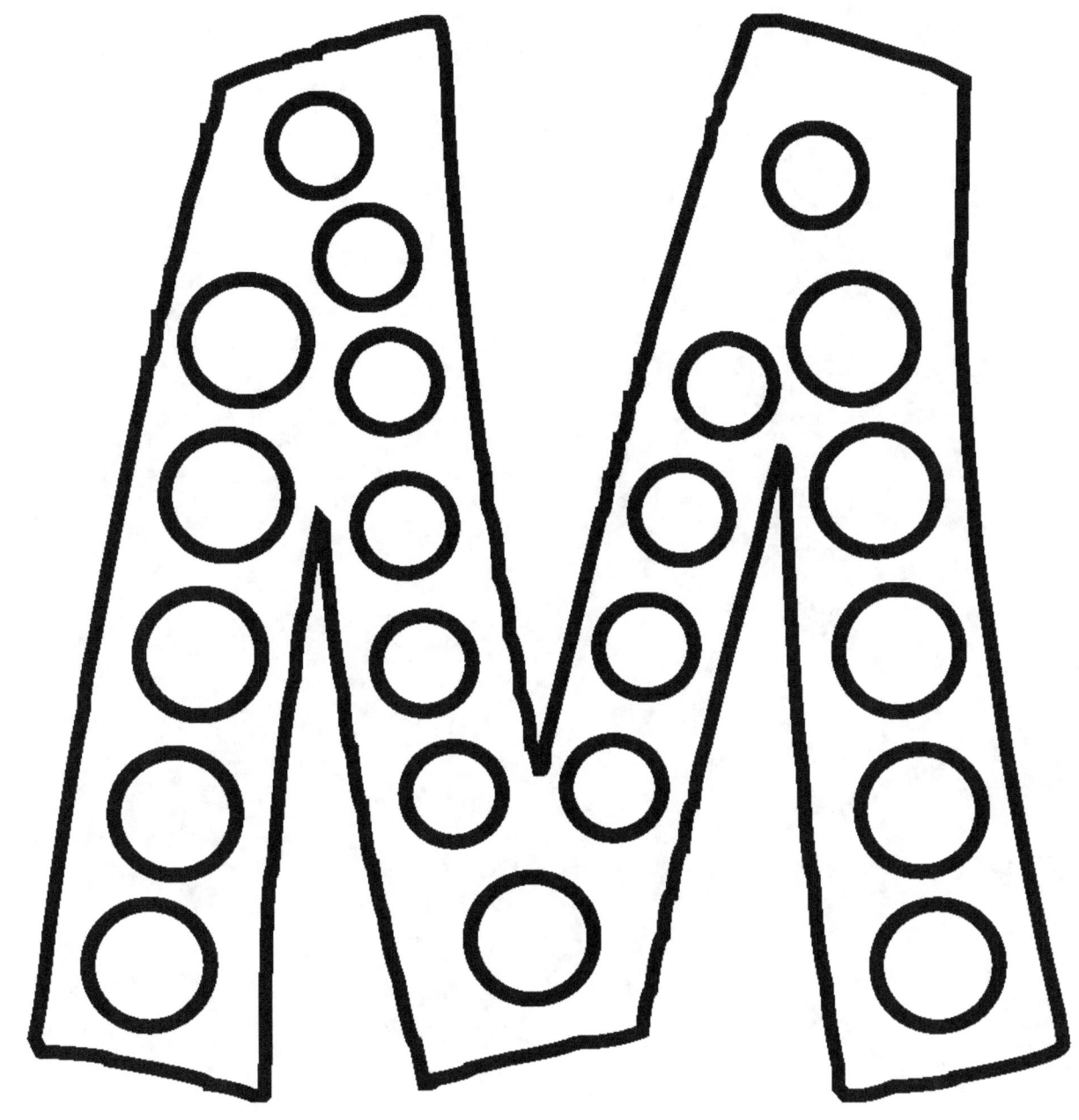

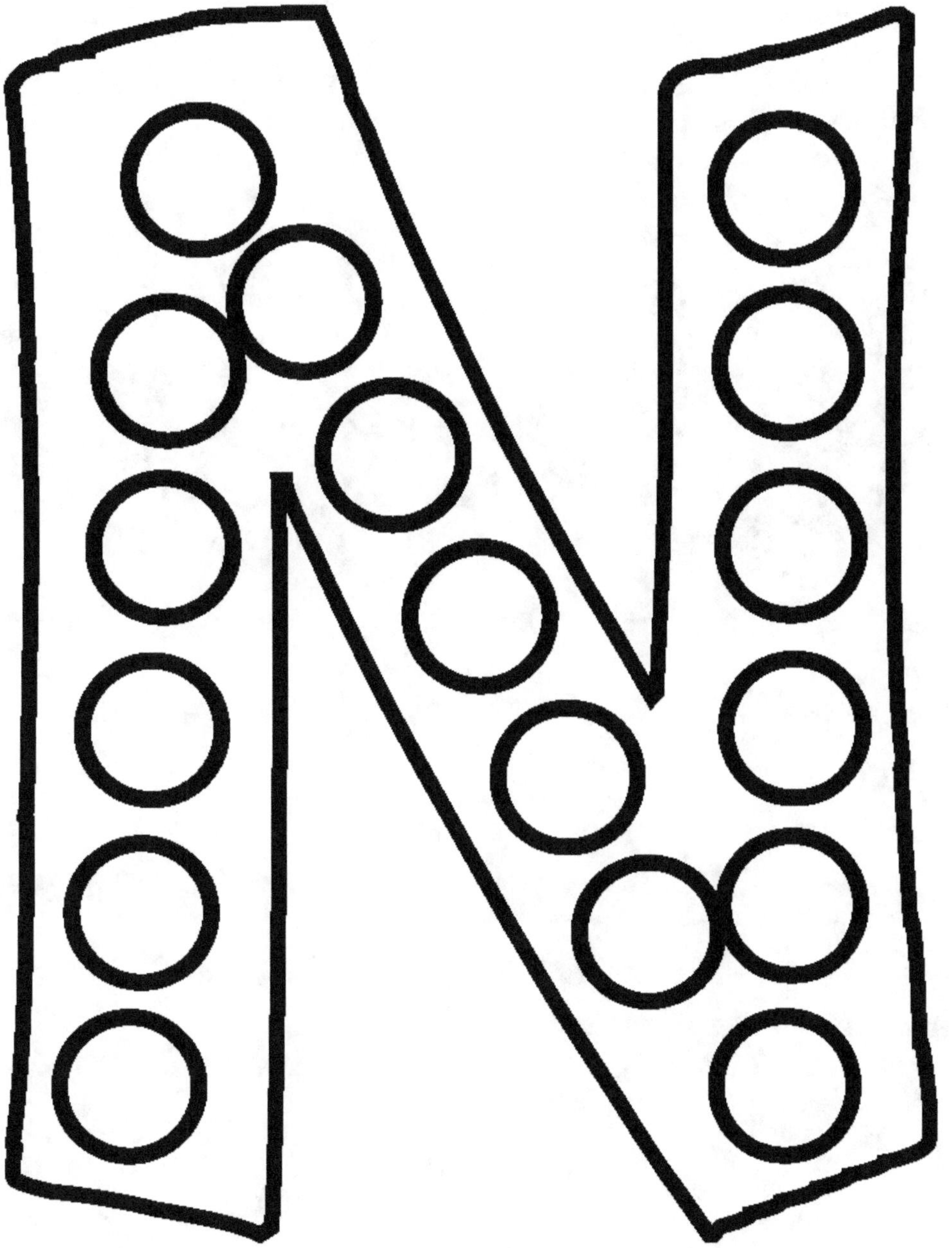

N

NARWHAL

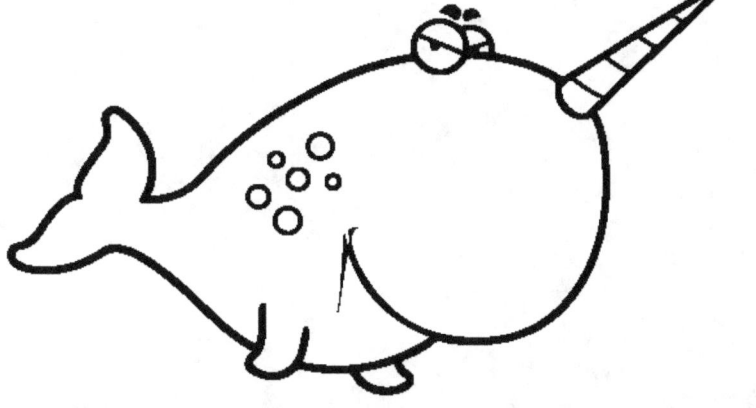

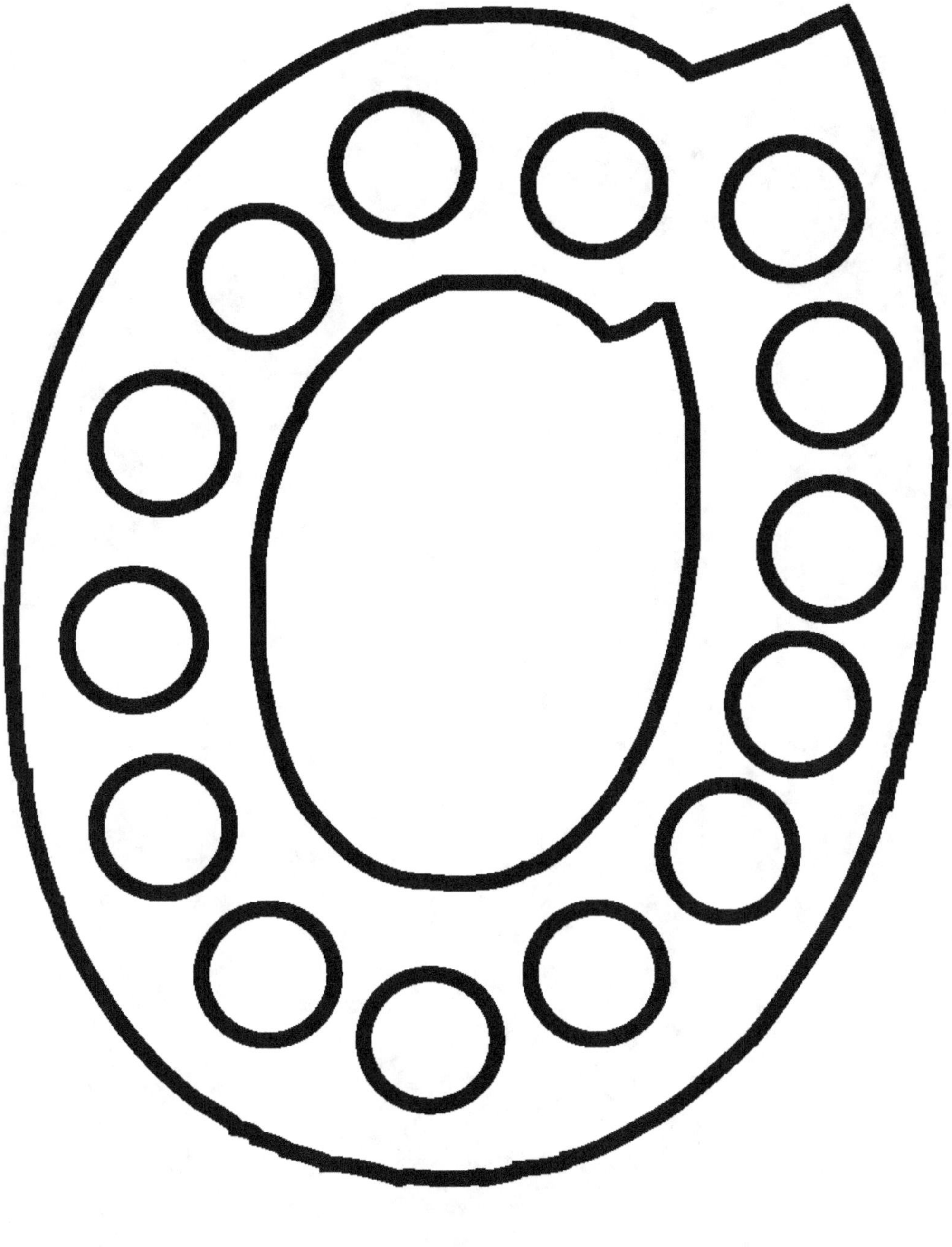

OCTOPUS

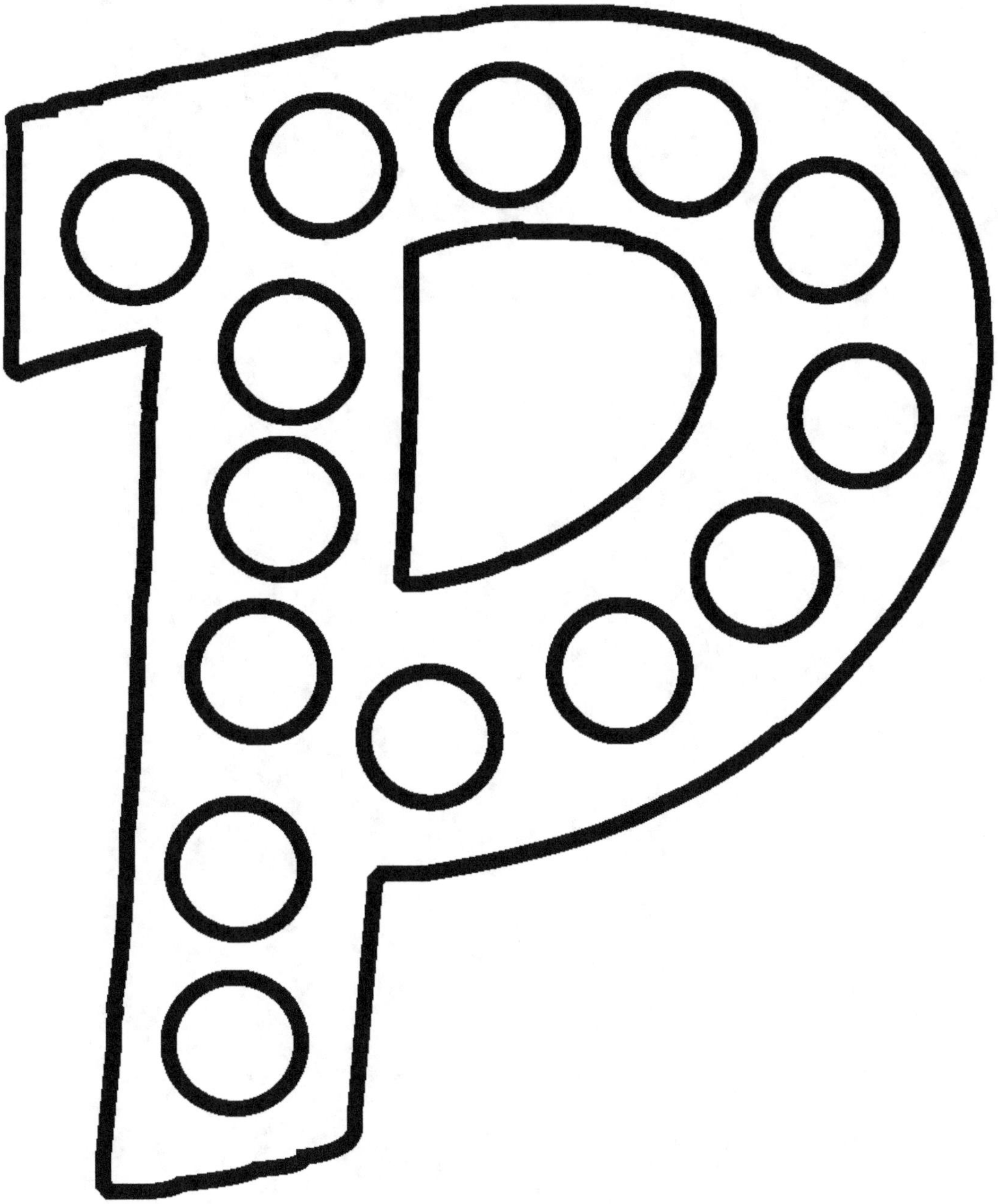

P

PIG

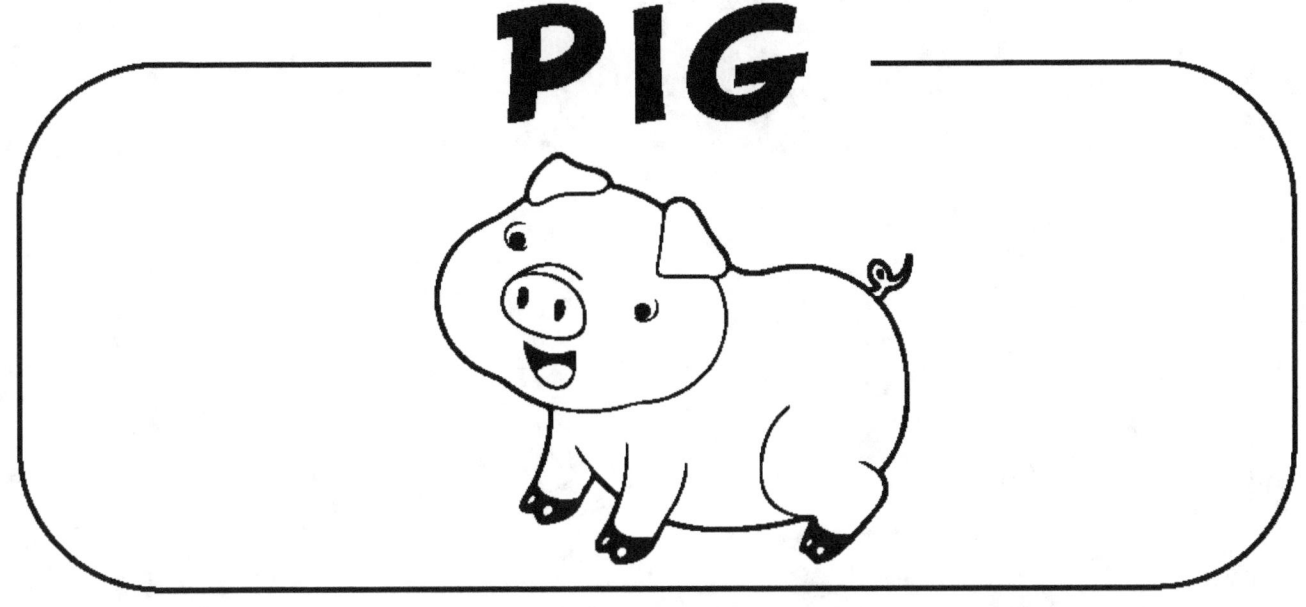

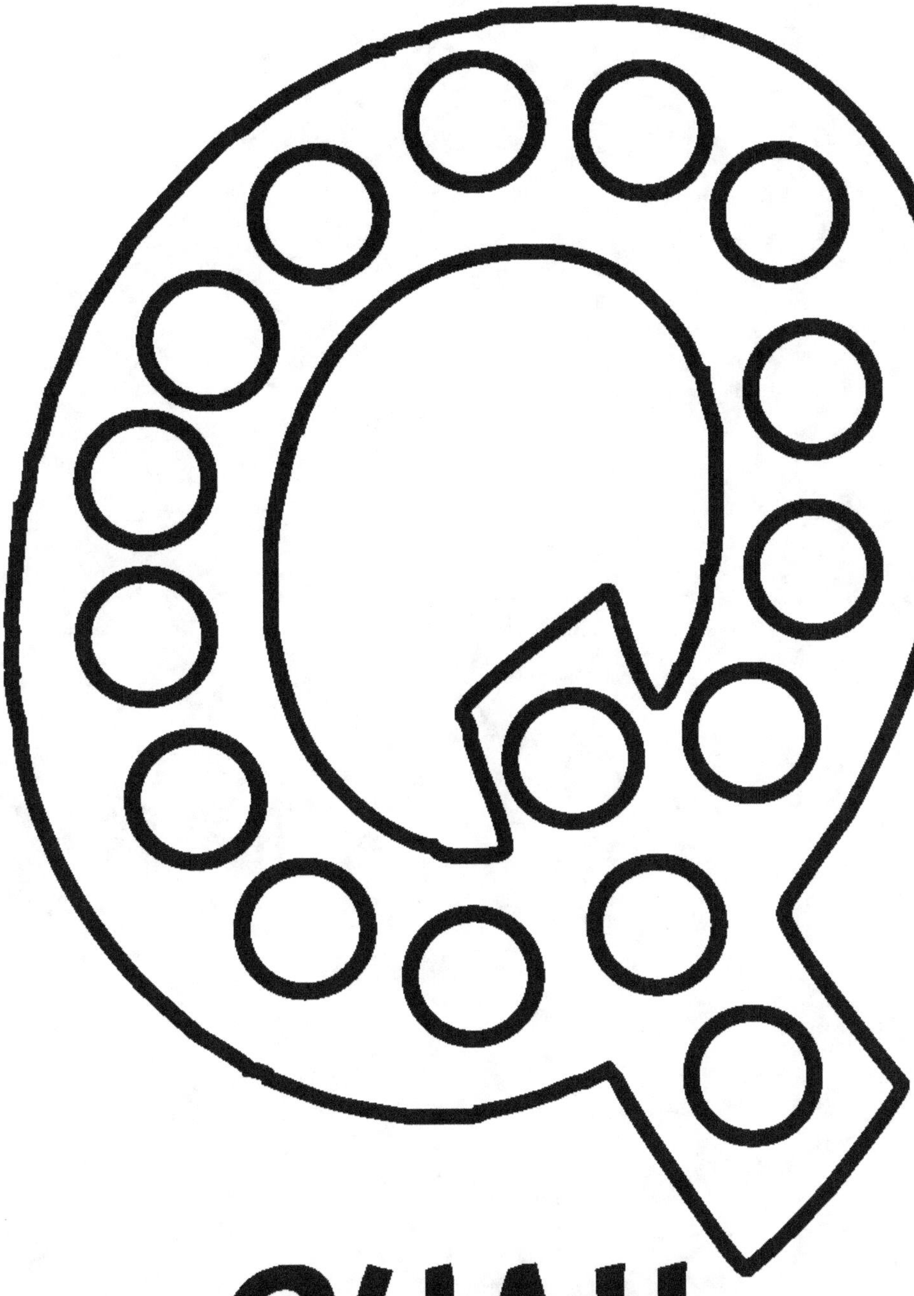

Q

QUAIL

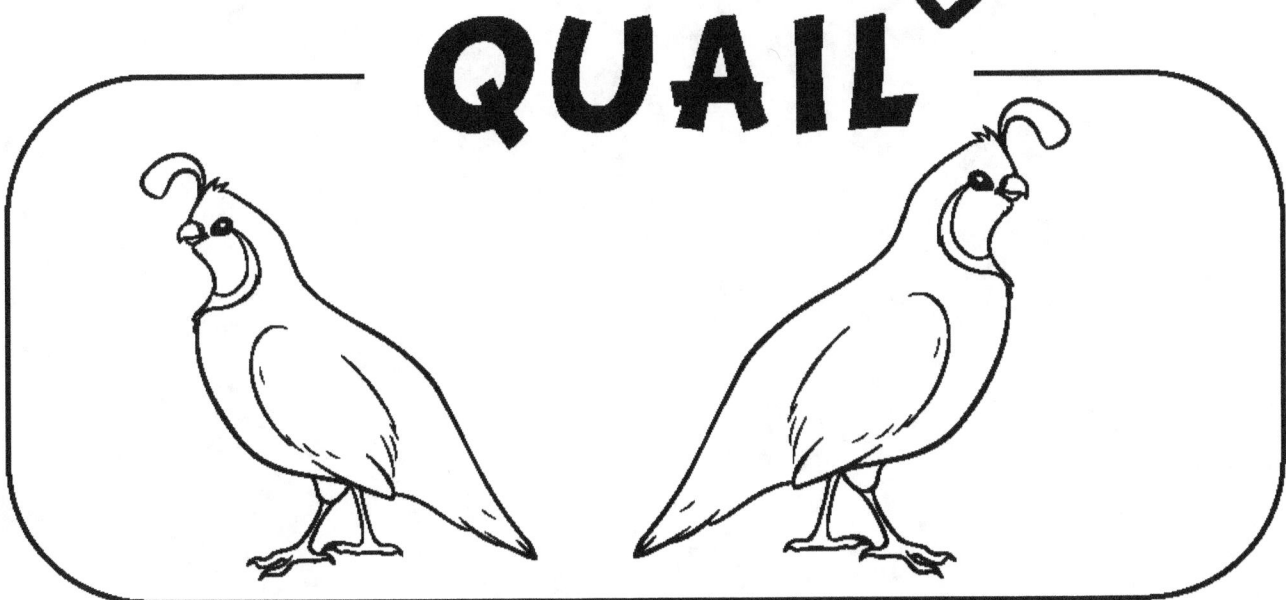

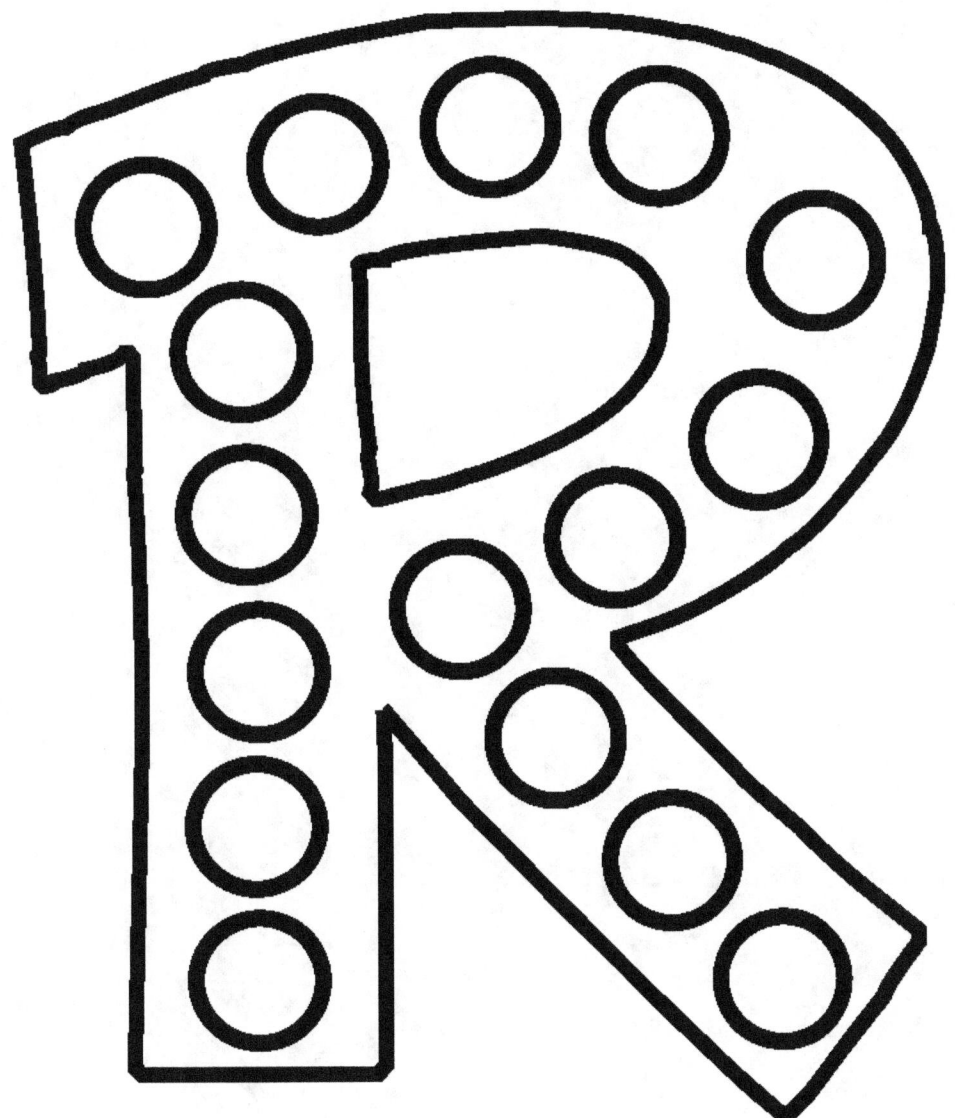

RABBIT

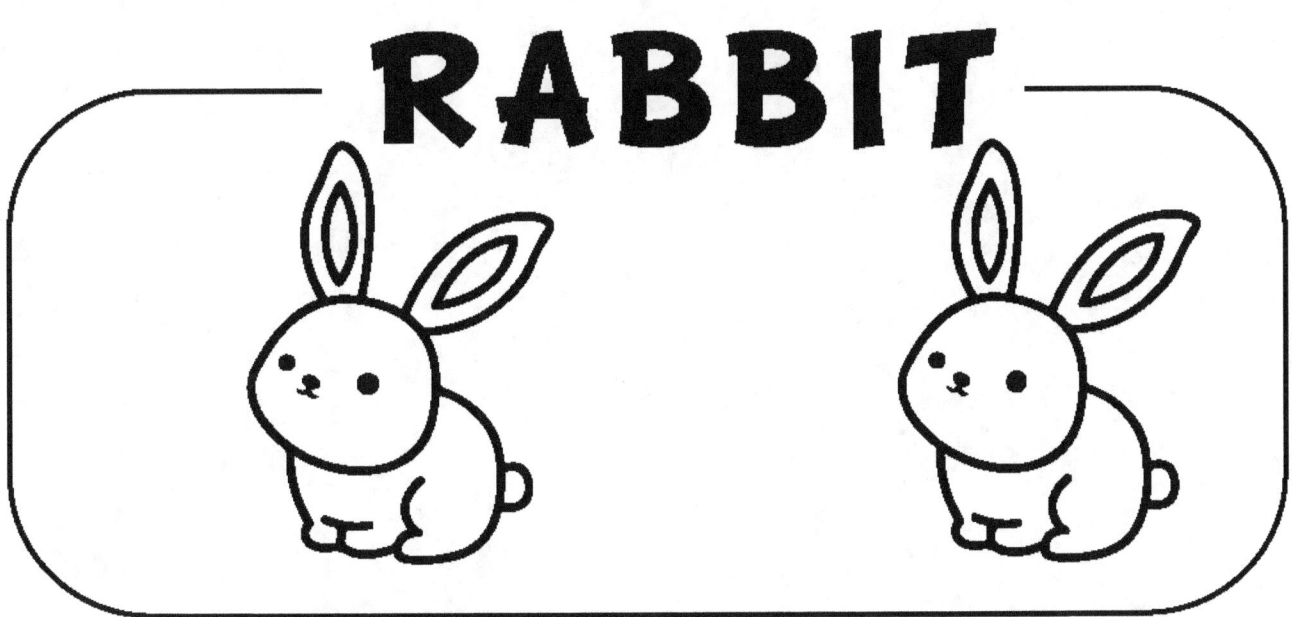

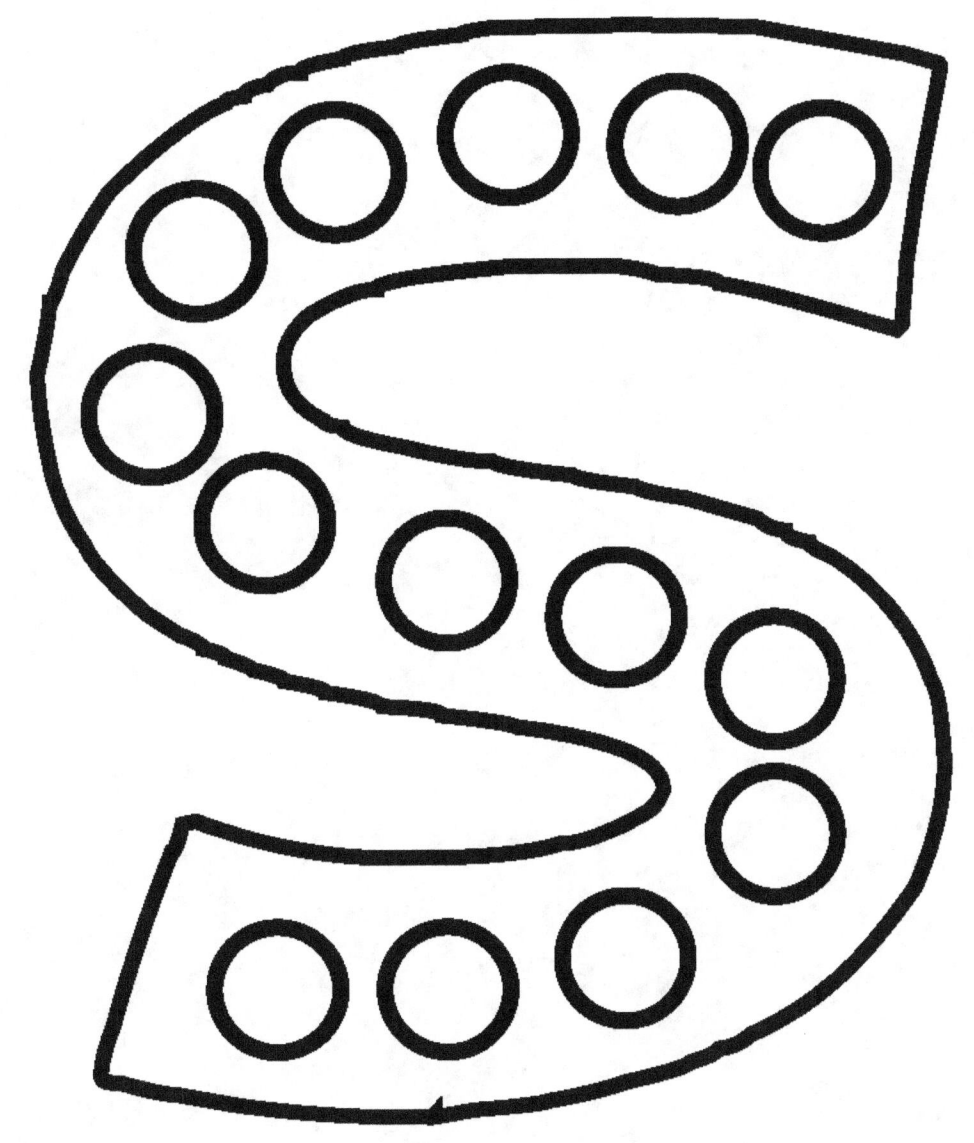

SNAKE

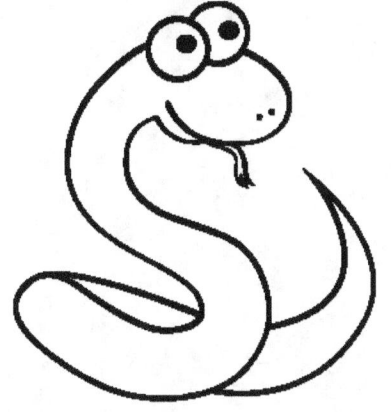

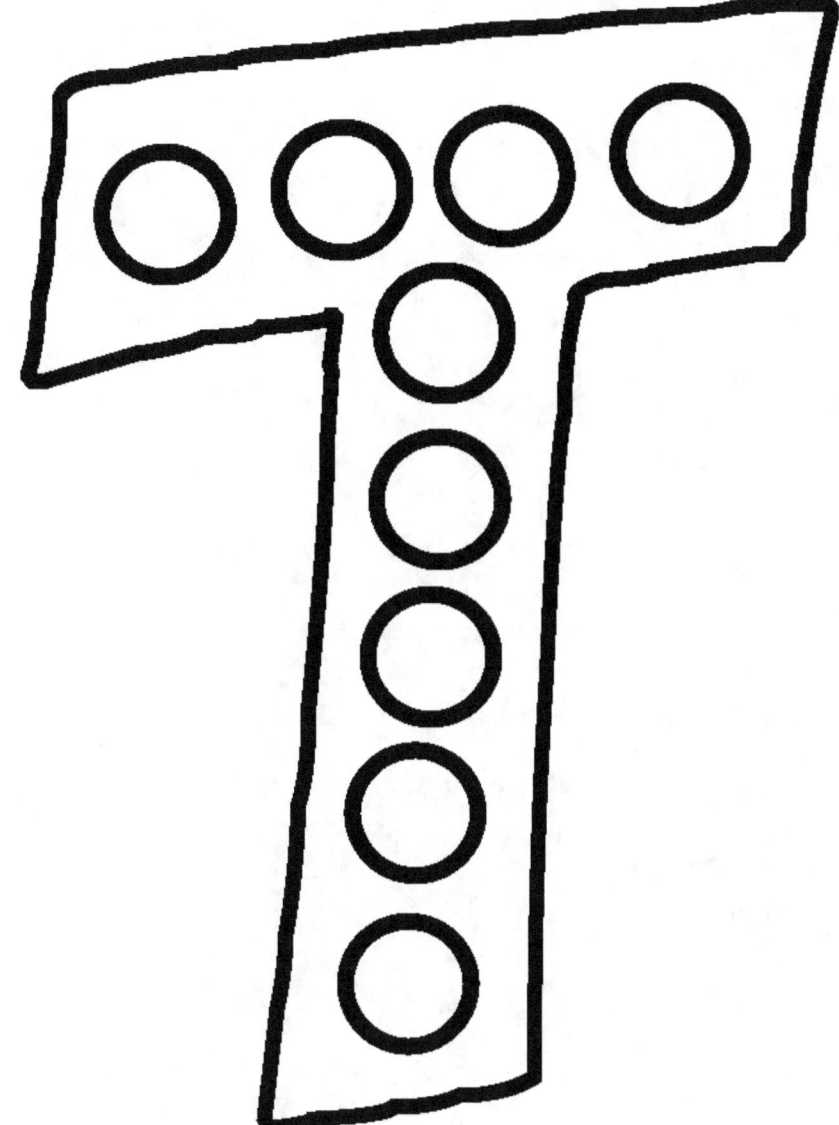

TURTLE

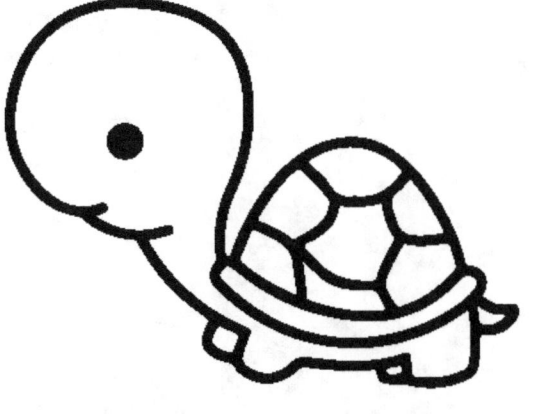

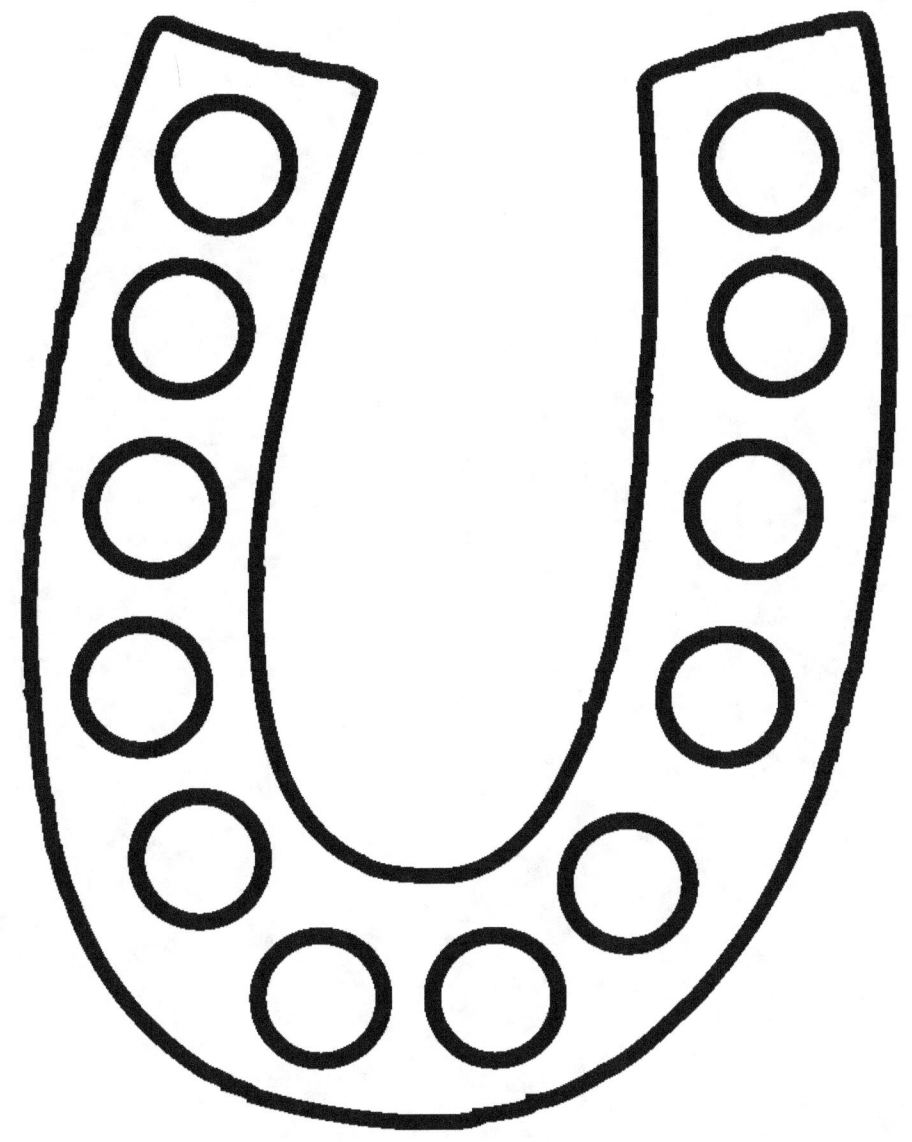

UNICORN

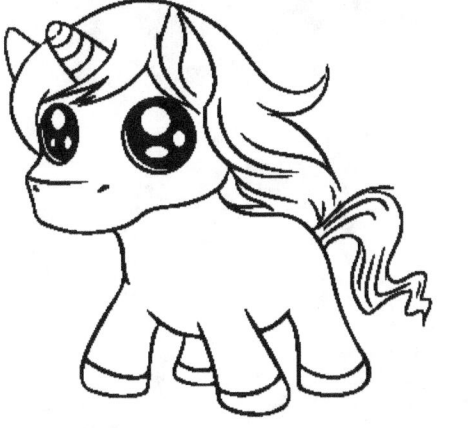

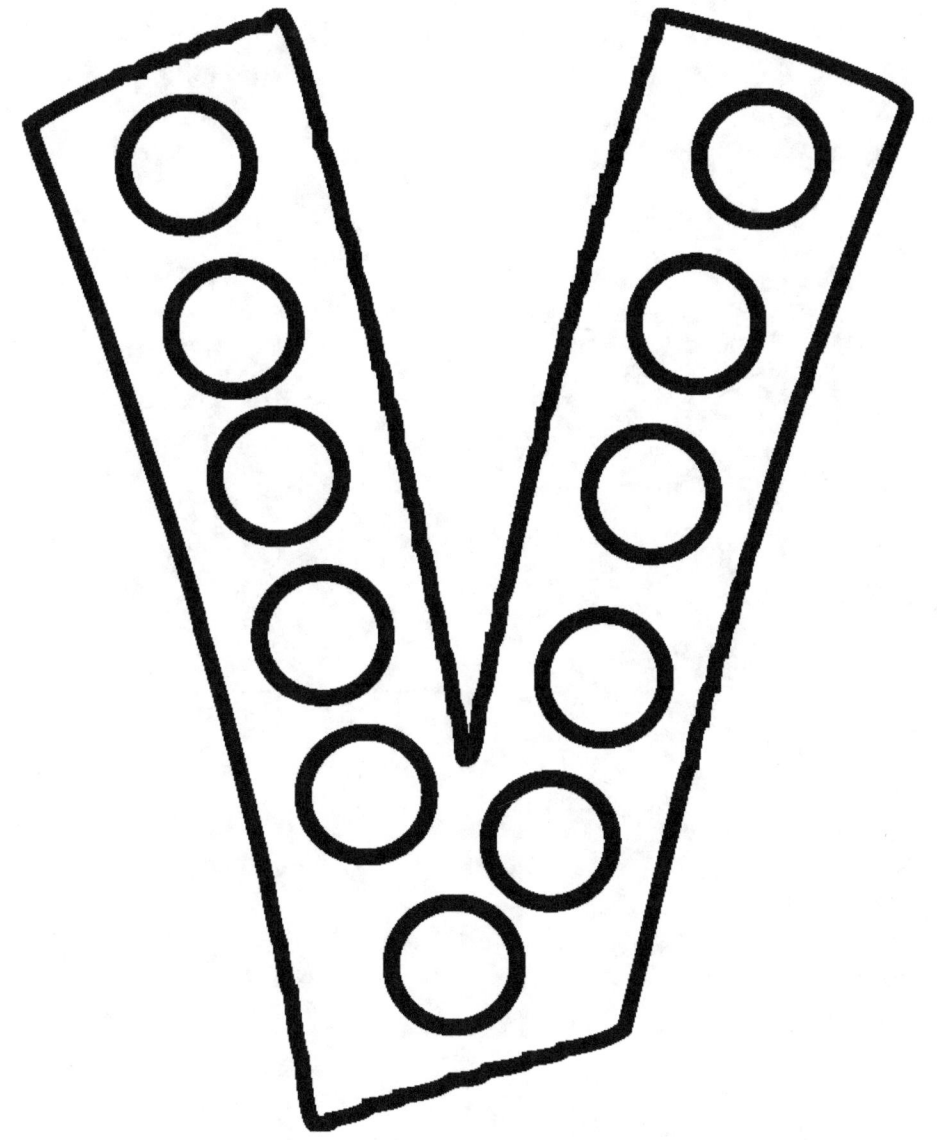

VULTURE

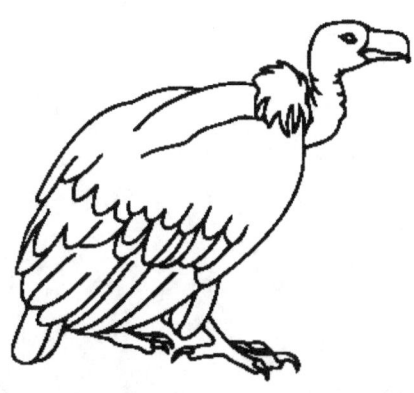

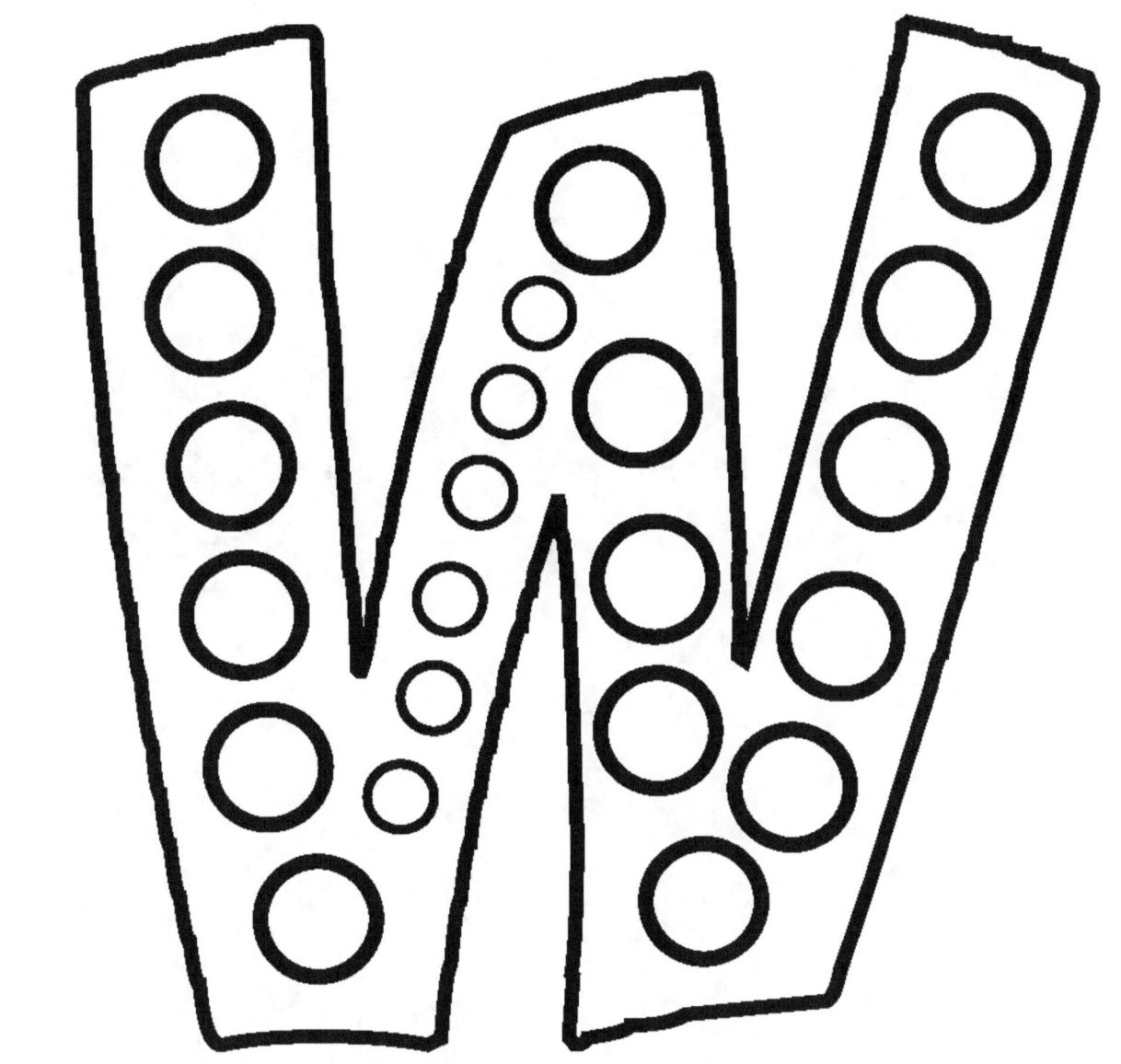

WOLF

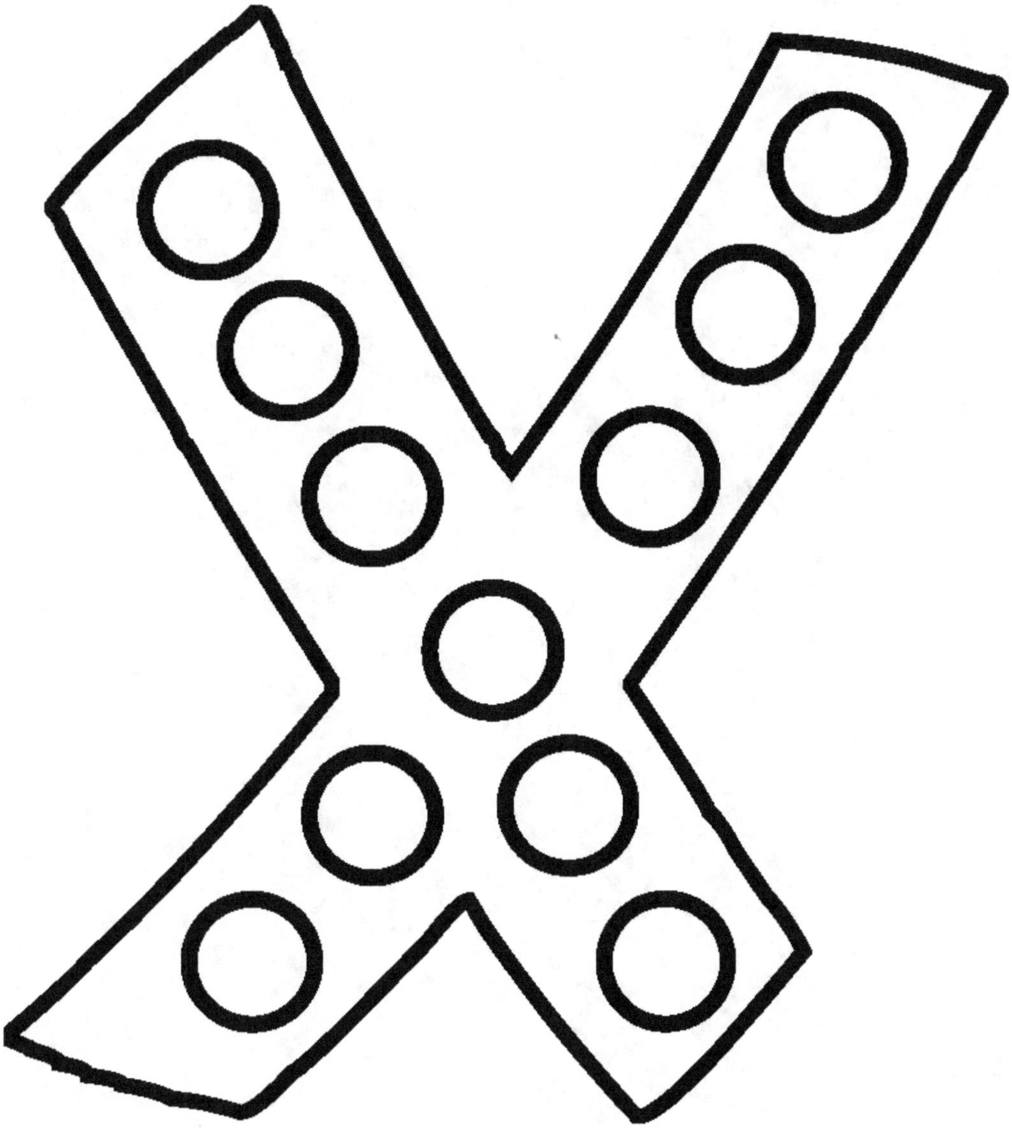

X

XERUS

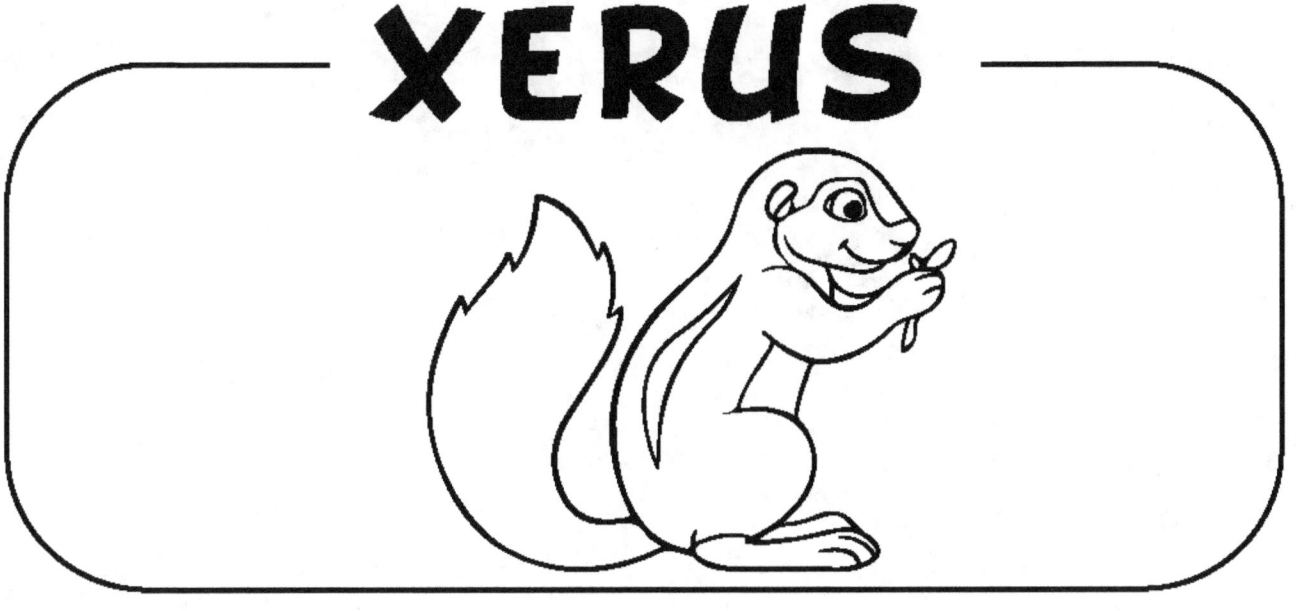

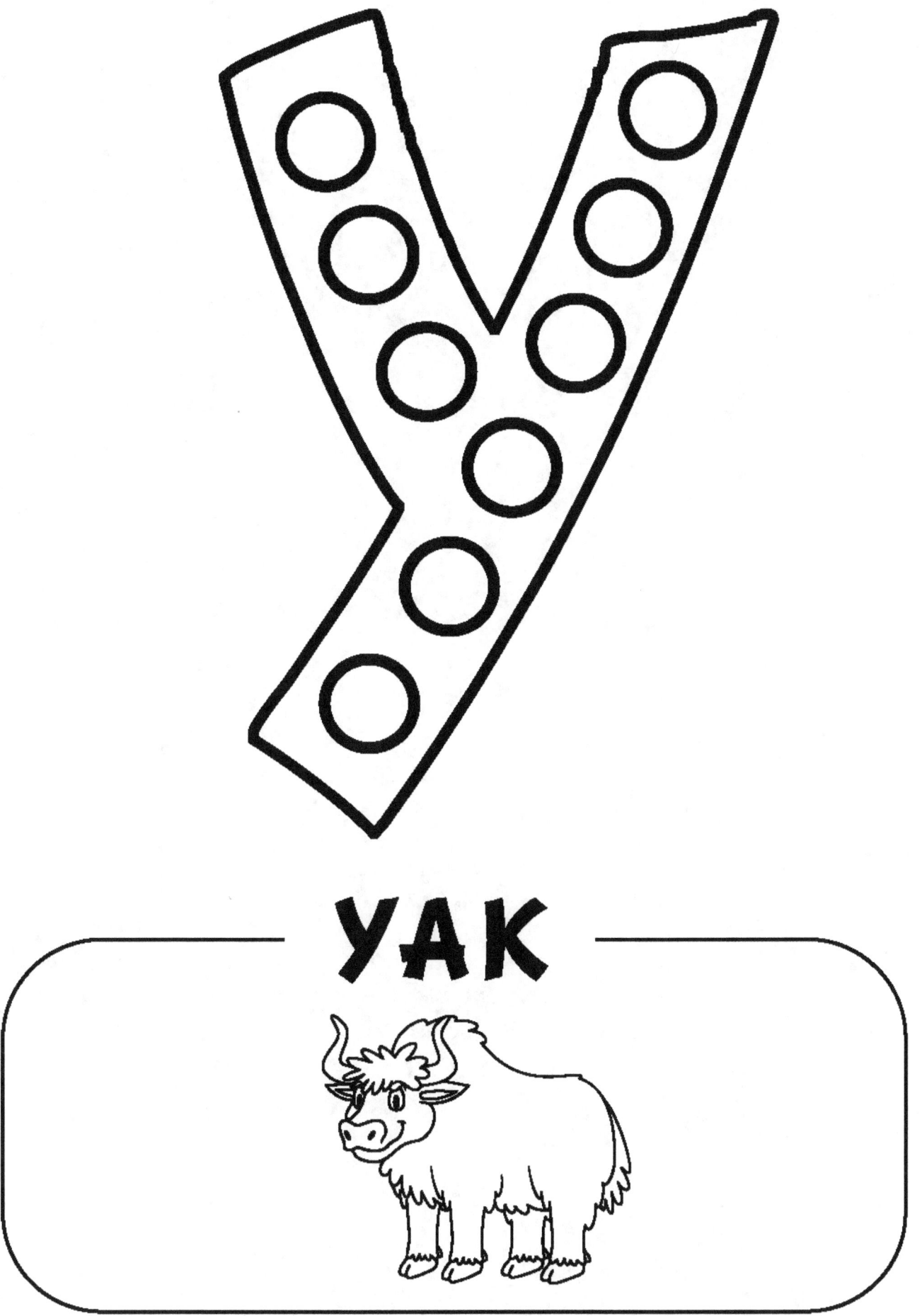

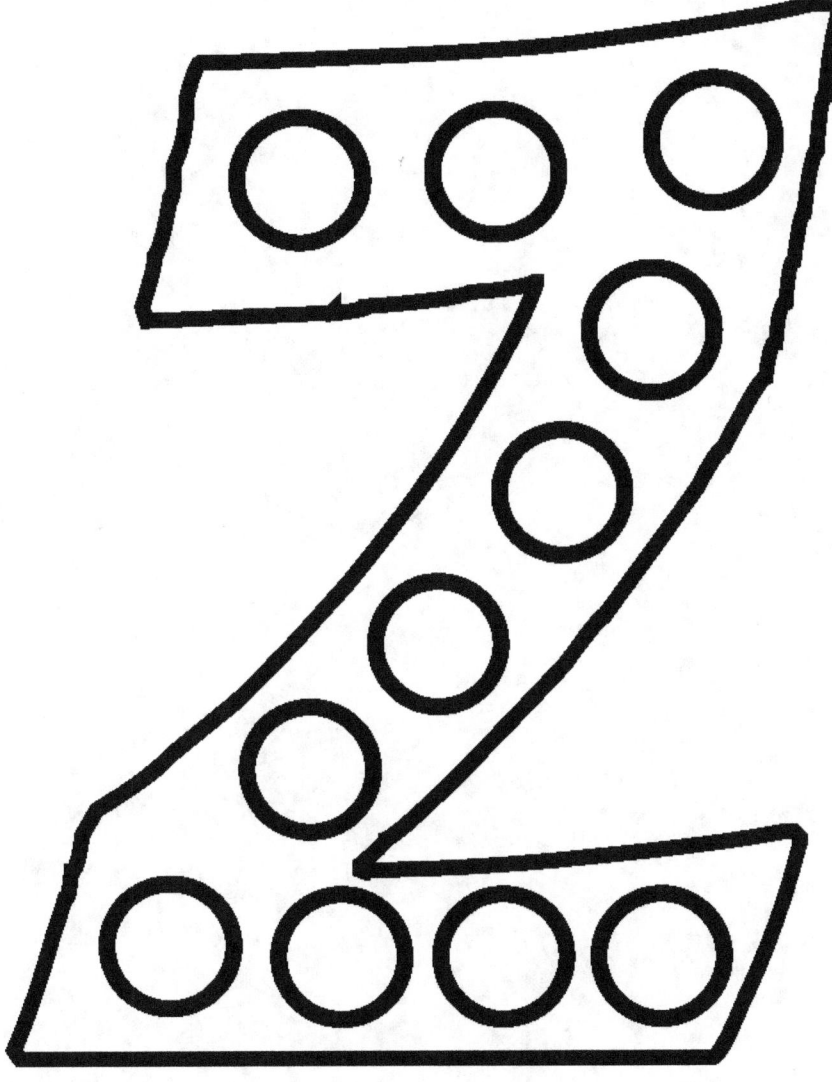

ZEBRA

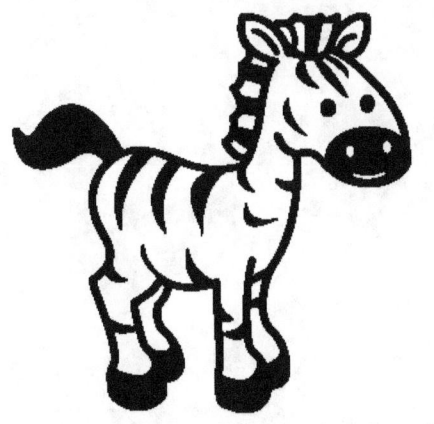

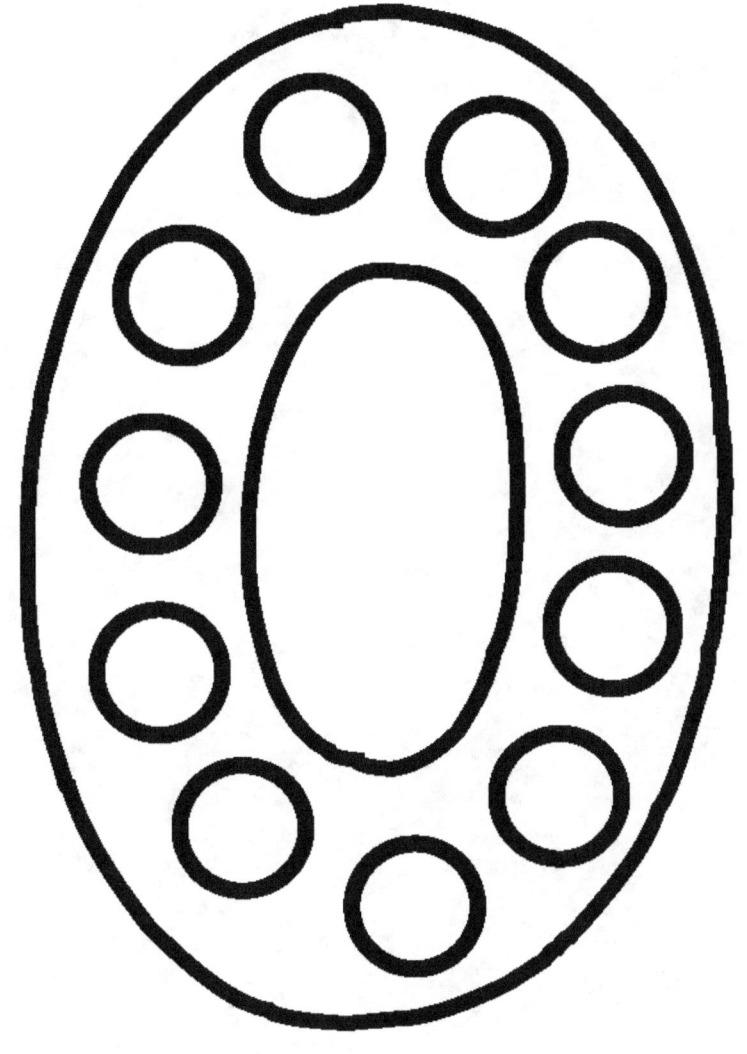

ZERO

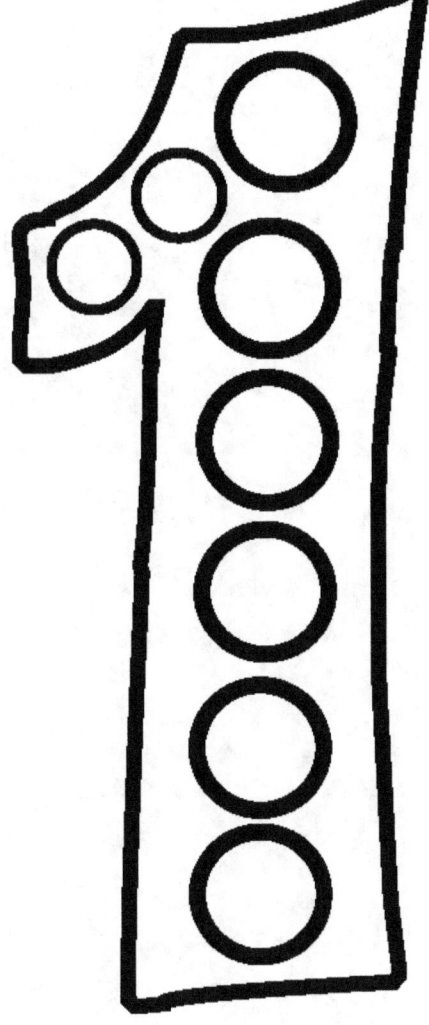

ONE

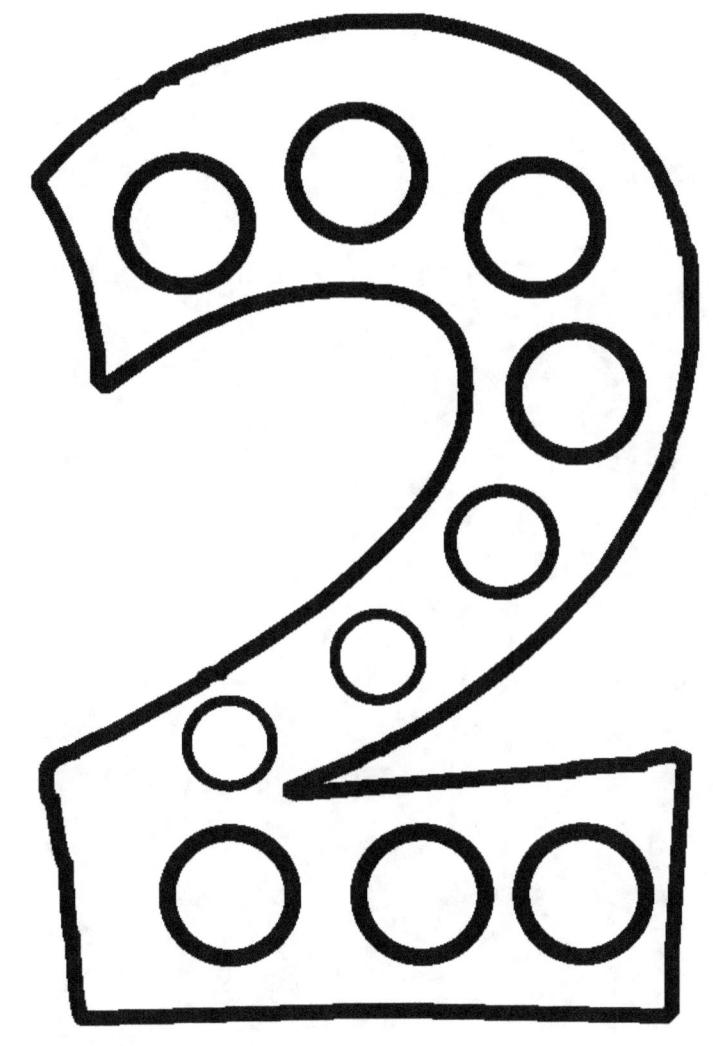

TWO

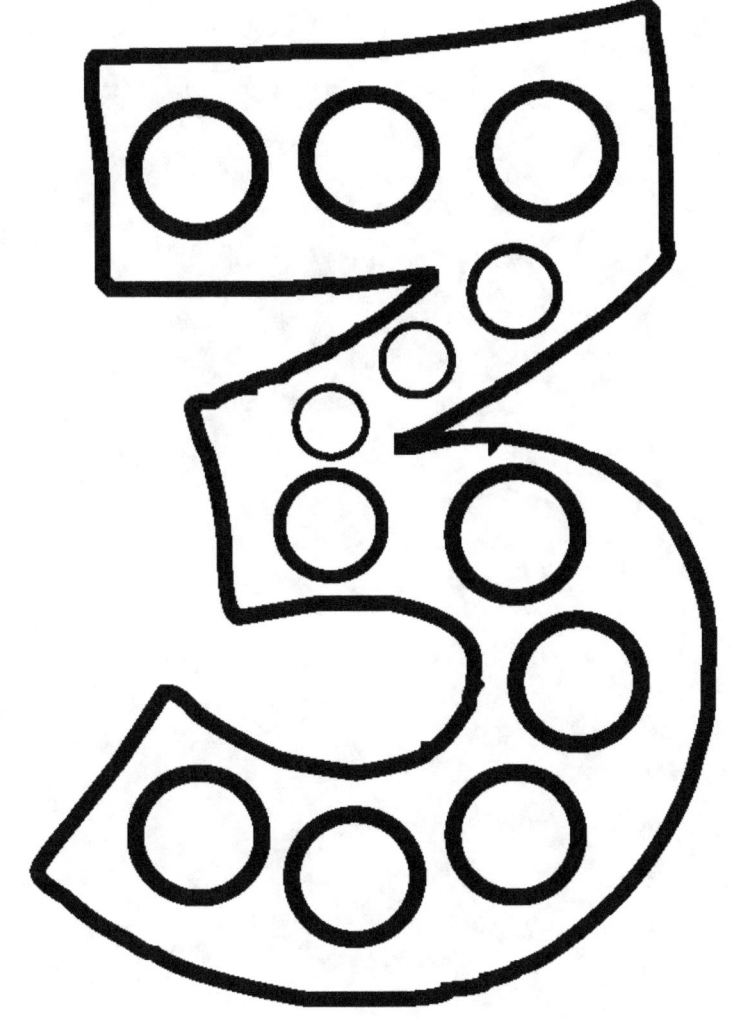

THREE

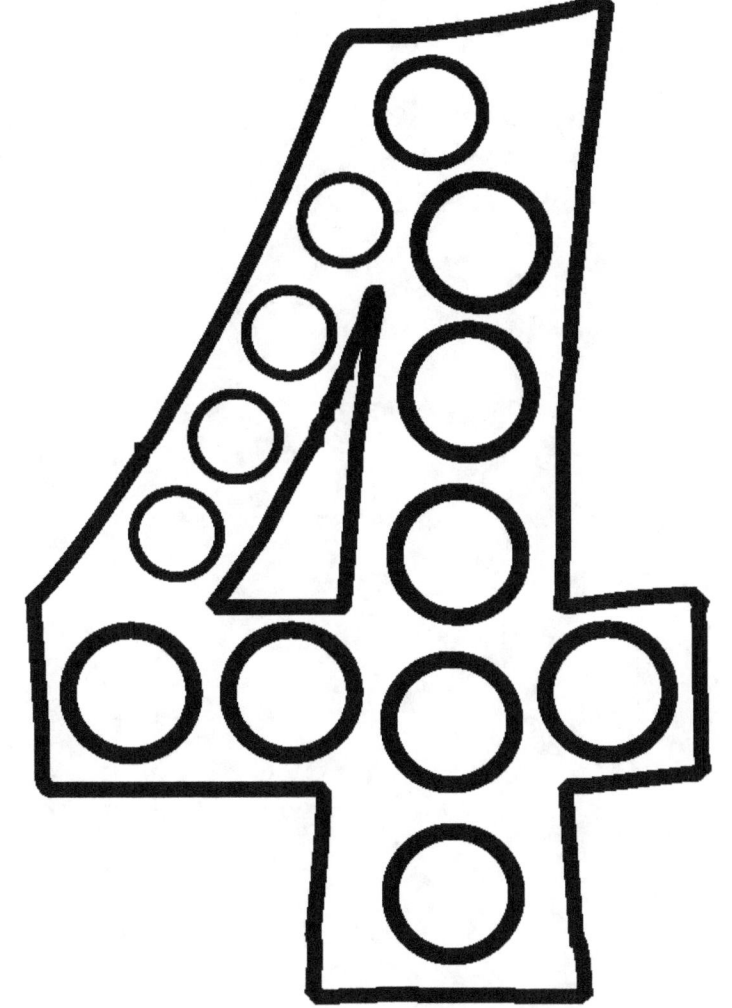

FOUR

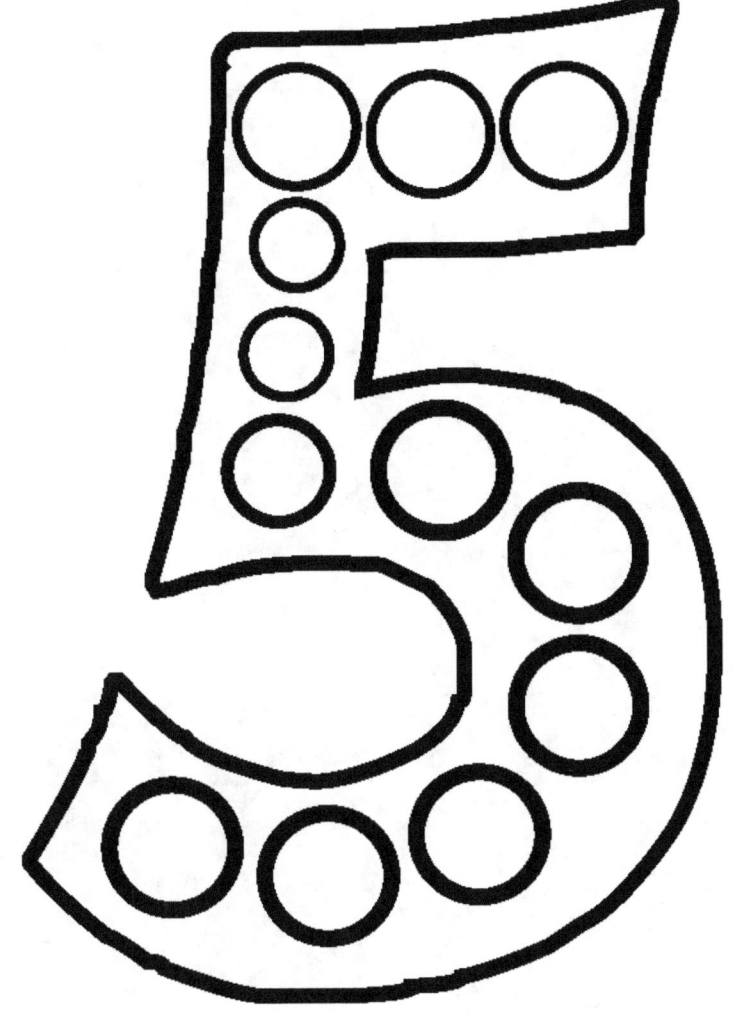

FIVE

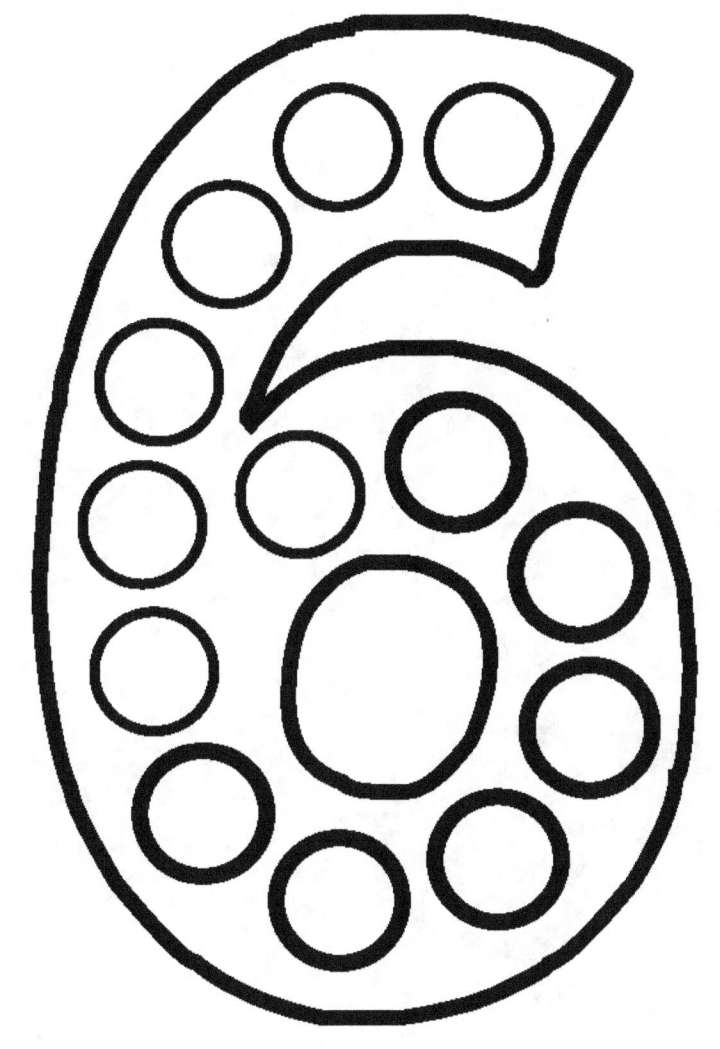

six

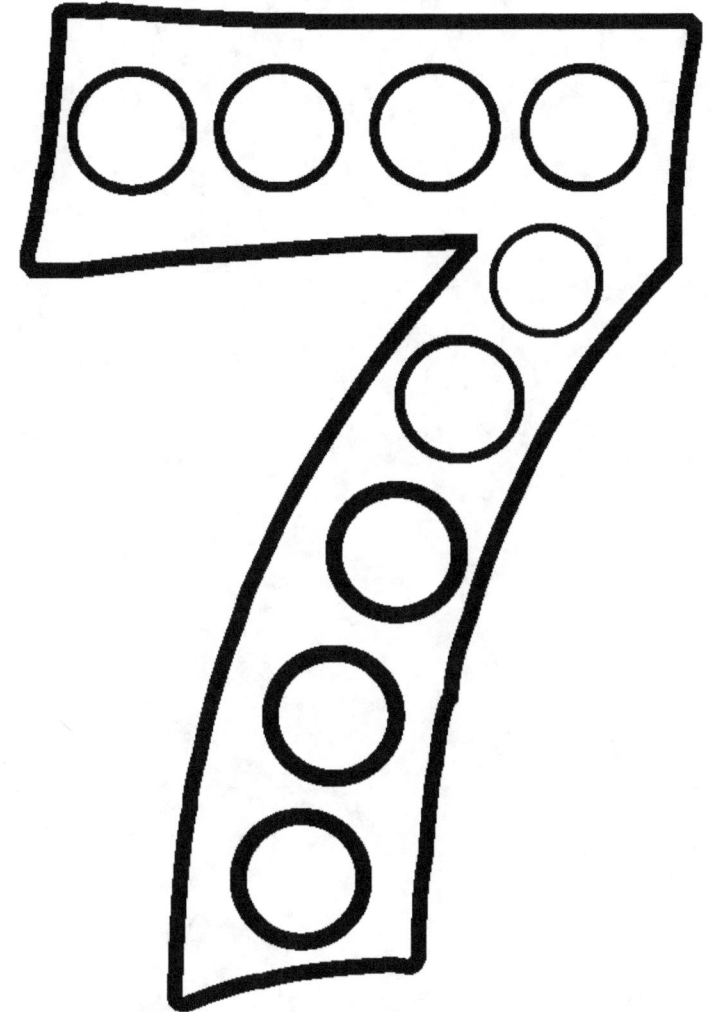

SEVEN

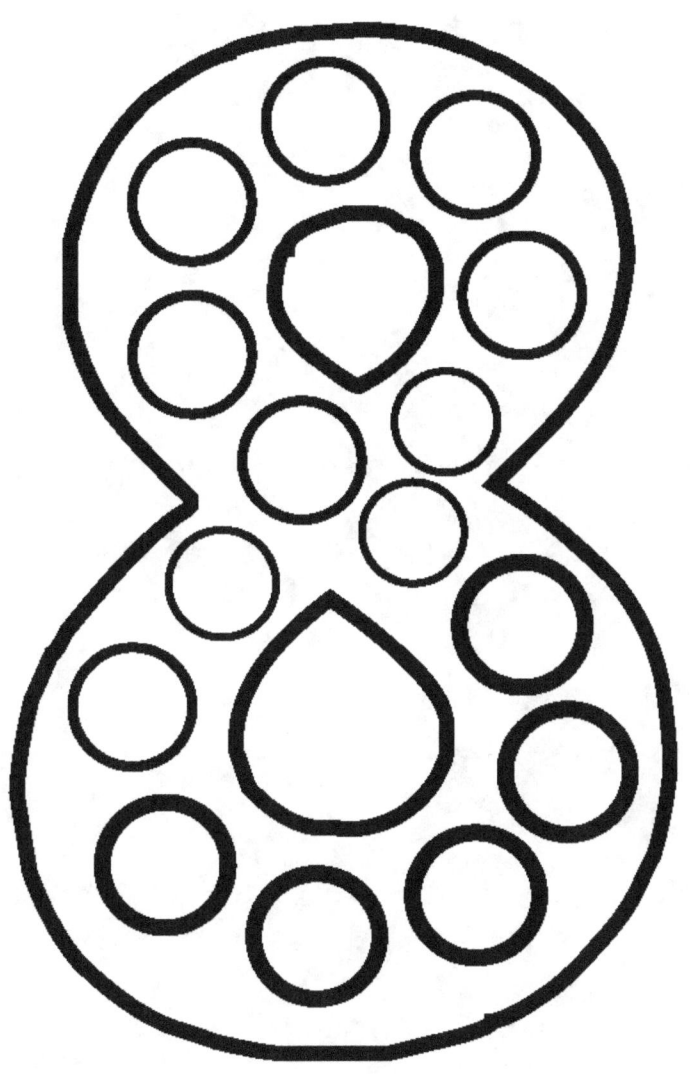

EiGHT

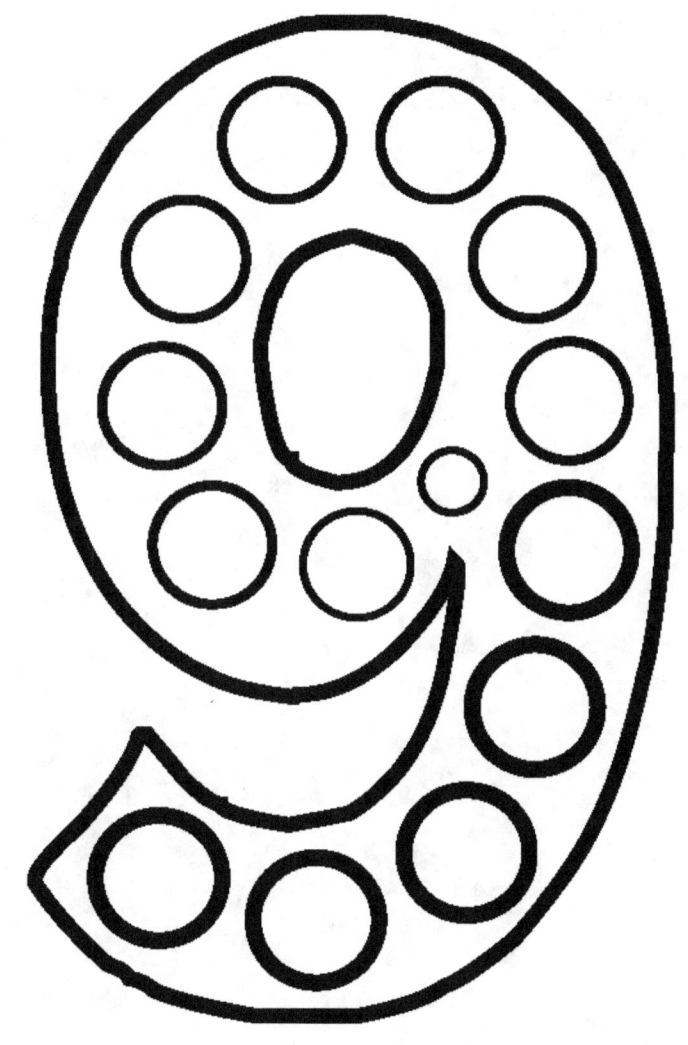

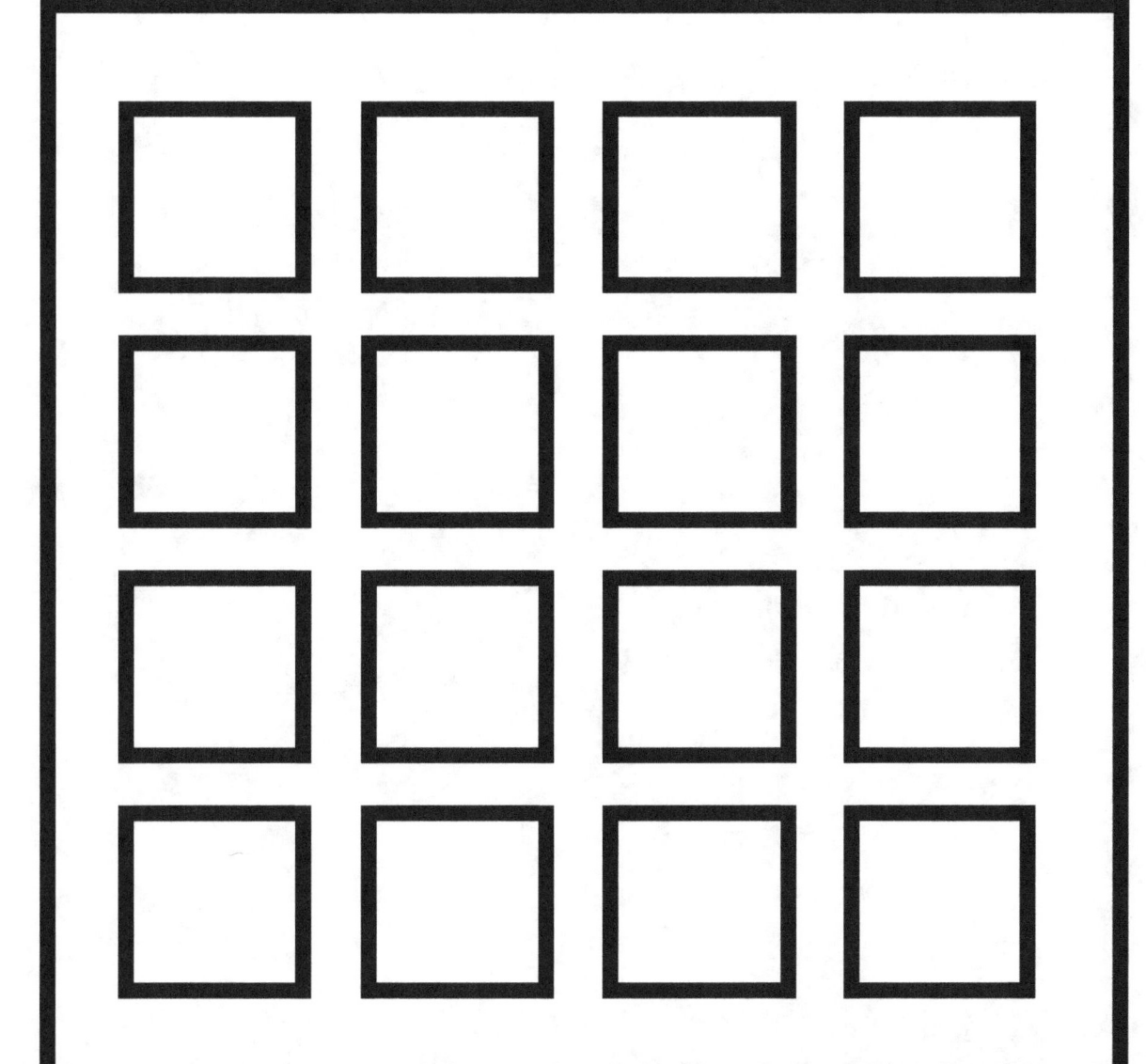

SQUARE

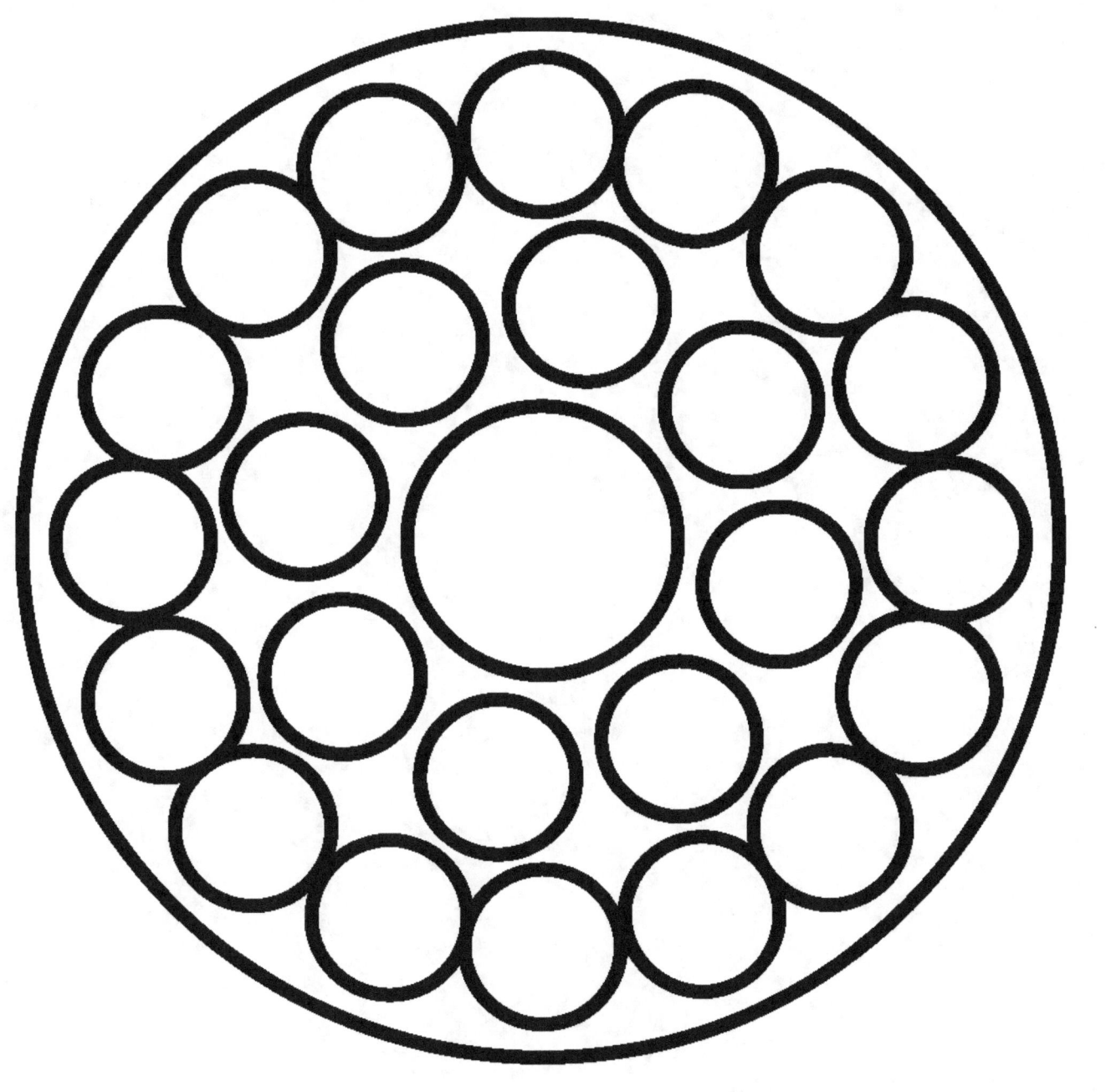

CIRCLE

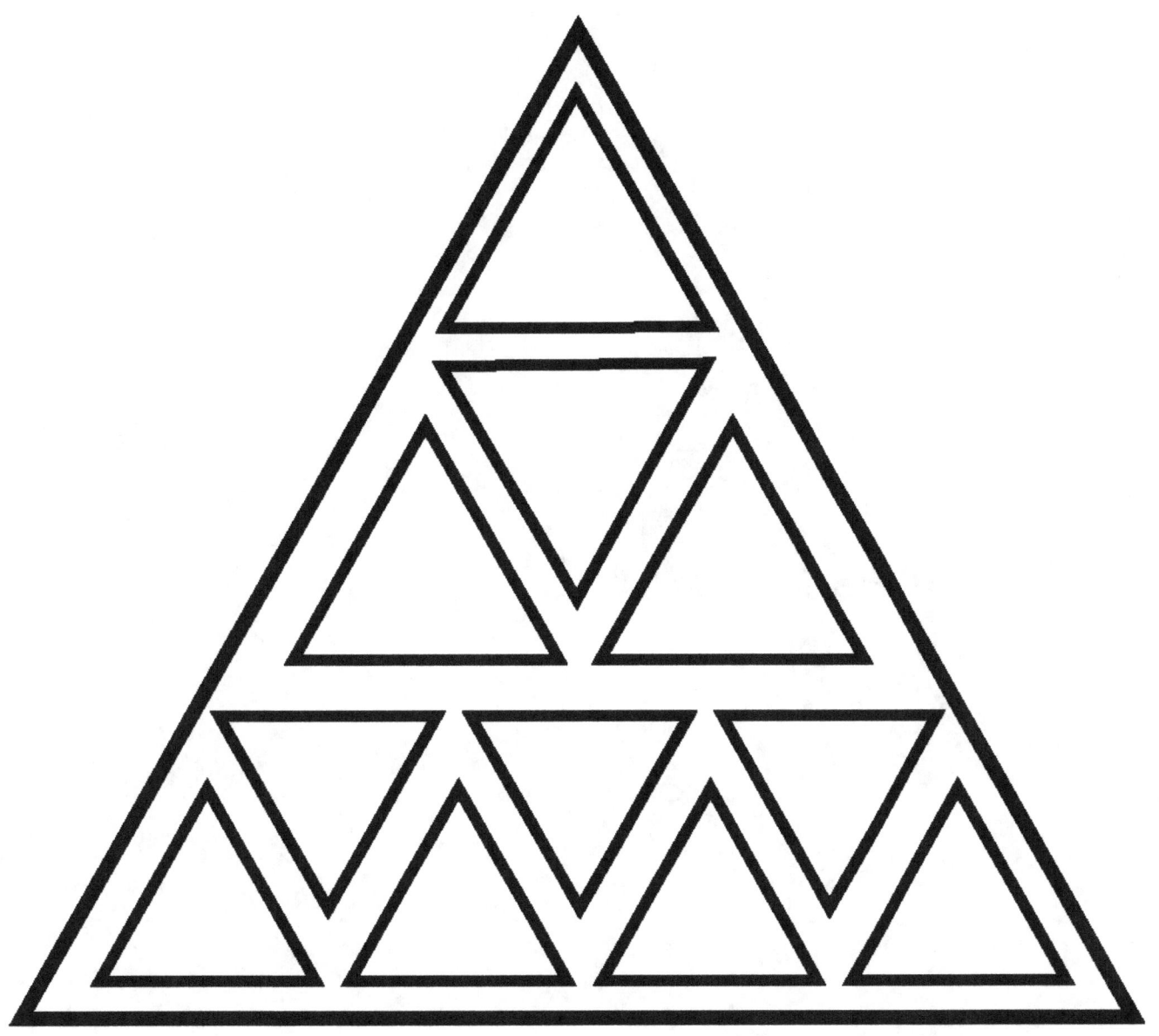

TRIANGLE

www.ingramcontent.com/pod-product-compliance
Lightning Source LLC
Chambersburg PA
CBHW080520220526
45465CB00006B/2540